DREAM GARDENS

Discovering the Gardens of the Lake District

Vivian Russell

CENTURY
London Sydney Auckland Johannesburg

My thanks to everyone all over Cumbria who opened their garden gates to me; to Rachael Polkinghorne, Donna McCrae and Jacqueline Jackson for allowing me to escape through ours unaccompanied by the patter of little feet; to Molly who coped valiantly with Rupert; to Sally Hamilton and Nanny B. who did the same for me; to Christine Compton and the RHS and Keswick Libraries for help with the words and Terry Warman, June Nash and St Martin's Studio for help with the pictures; to Fred Holdsworth and Stan Holland for being in the right place at the right time; and to Ken, for all sorts of things – like a one-way ticket to Borrowdale, constancy – and Kodachrome.

First published in 1989 by Century Hutchinson Ltd,
Brookmount House, 62-65 Chandos Place, Covent Garden,
London WC2N 4NW

Century Hutchinson Australia Pty Ltd, 89-91 Albion Street,
Surry Hills, Sydney, New South Wales 2010, Australia

Century Hutchinson New Zealand Limited, PO Box 40-086,
Glenfield, Auckland 10, New Zealand

Century Hutchinson South Africa (Pty) Ltd, PO Box 337,
Bergvlei, 2012 South Africa

Book design by Bob Hook

Set in 11/16 Baskerville
by SX Composing Ltd, Rayleigh, Essex

Printed and bound in Great Britain by Butler & Tanner, Frome.

British Library Cataloguing in Publication Data
Russell, Vivian
Dream gardens. Discovering the gardens of the Lake District.
1. Cumbria. Gardens open to the public.
Visitors' guides
I. Title
914.27'804858

ISBN 0-7126-2912-2

....

(PREVIOUS PAGE) CHERUB BY DAN GIBSON,
GRAYTHWAITE HALL

....

CONTENTS

To all who garden in Cumbria –
those that live in houses
and those that don't

FOREWORD

by Ken Russell

I arrived in Cumbria for the first time one blustery winter's night in 1965. Tucked away in the north-west corner of England, Cumbria was a place we southerners usually bypassed on our way to Scotland. Until I read about it while researching a subject I planned to film, I barely knew of its existence. That all changed the moment I drew the curtains in my hotel bedroom the next morning and saw the most breathtaking sight of my life. It was a revelation. I was in Paradise – and determined to stay there as long as possible. To that end I've dragged film crews up its hills and down its dales ever since. As Delius composed 'The Song of the High Hills' and Roger Daltrey sang 'Listening to you I hear the music', the fells were alive with the sound of playback.

My appreciation of the wonders of Lakeland were greatly enhanced by the magnificent books of A. J. Wainwright, which are indispensable guides for those wishing to climb the mountain of their choice by the path with the most glorious views. Wainwright is one of nature's philosophers and, when it comes to a knowledge and understanding of the Lake District, I always thought he'd had the last word. And then I opened this book – and experienced another revelation. Here was a world Wainwright had never mentioned and I'd never dreamed of.

The poet Coleridge once called Skiddaw (the mountain I saw through that hotel window over thirty years ago) God, made manifest. Here in this book are the dreams and aspirations of His children made manifest – children of all ages who, through love and endeavour, have each created in the paradise in which we live a little Eden for all of us to share.

O happy Garden! whose seclusion deep
Hath been so friendly to industrious hours;
And to soft slumbers, that did gently steep
Our spirits, carrying with them dreams of flowers,
And wild notes warbled among leafy bowers
WILLIAM WORDSWORTH

I N T R O D U C T I O N

U n d e r   t h e   R a i n b o w

Every gardener is a dreamer and the Lake District is a particularly good place to dream in. People have been dreaming here for years and making their dreams come true. Wordsworth did it in poetry, Beatrix Potter for children, Ruskin for art, Turner on canvas, Wainwright for walkers, Ken Russell on film, and Hugh Walpole, Arthur Ransome and Melvyn Bragg between hard covers.

Another group of artists, those who paint with flower and foliage on a detail of a canvas that reaches to the horizon, have also created masterpieces. But they are of a fleeting and vulnerable kind. The kind you can't bring in from the rain or protect from the wind. The kind you never finish. The kind you can't sell copies of or put under the auctioneer's hammer and ship off to Japan. The only realized work of art that doesn't increase in value yet gives pleasure to thousands. It's a lifetime's work and one that dies with you. A garden.

No one is more closely involved with the living face of Cumbria than the humble gardener. He gets all the rain and little of the glory. The lakes and mountains have had it all, dwarfing by their grandeur the subtler beauty of what lies below, including the quiet radiance of rural Cumbria. But if you step back into even the simplest of gardens and look again, how much richer the view. The gardens of the Lake District are, after all, only gardens within a larger, wilder garden. But before you can create a garden in a landscape as forceful as this you have first to experience it.

When I first came here eleven years ago to start a new life the fells were also the first to catch my imagination. I had skiied the Alps, awesome but intimidating, toured the wide, bleak expanse of Scotland and lived amongst the hills of New England, so thickly wooded you could never see their shape. But I had never seen mountains like these: every contour exposed, every peak accessible within a day. I climbed them, a diminutive citizen of Lilliput in a large, surrealist rock garden, always aware of the many footsteps before mine. Foresters, smelters, farmers and miners had over the years smoothed the mountains over. The farmers built stone walls which swept down the fells across the valleys and up again, knitting the whole landscape together. Harnessed but not tamed, it was divided into asymmetrical plots, tended by sheep, our earliest landscape gardeners. Heather, gorse and bracken they allowed and everything else they ate.

It took me several years before I'd absorbed this extended garden sufficiently to look at our own. I couldn't really feel part of a place whose soil I hadn't worked, forking

OUR LOCAL DECORATOR'S BACK GARDEN
UNDER SKIDDAW

it over and planting things. That became an all-consuming task and I thought of nothing else. But once a garden as small as ours is planted and launched the great burst of creativity is over. I had always loved looking at other people's gardens and I loved looking at them more than ever as mine became ever more a family garden. Why are secateurs so much more exciting to a child of two than a sandbox?

The British are great enthusiasts and I think enthusiasm is the key to a happy life. This is a country with a gardening tradition we Americans have long envied, one that had overwhelmed me. And I wanted to know more about it. It seemed to me we did not hear nearly enough about how the ordinary gardener felt about his garden, what it meant to him, how it influenced him, and where it had all started. I wanted to bring the gardener back into focus and I wanted particularly for people to experience Cumbria through its gardens. I wanted gardens that looked quintessentially Cumbrian using scenery, architecture and people. Even a garden of just one flower set against this landscape makes a strange and haunting image.

Everyone always thinks of the Lake District when they hear of Cumbria but outside it lies the last frontier of England. In this rural and undiscovered paradise people

A ONE-LILY GARDEN IN THE
LOWESWATER LANDSCAPE

JOHN ROPER IN HIS FRONT GARDEN

still garden on the roadside and, failing that, the pavement doorstep instead of hiding their plants away behind a wall. It's a marvellous gift to anyone passing by. It lights up a village and is an act of faith that everyone respects except the sheep. It was in the heart of this area that I found John Roper, retired farmer, leaning against his farm wall one September morning staring at the clouds. He took in my practised introduction about this book without comment and posed quietly, though I can't really say he posed because he stared at the camera as imperturbably as he had stared at the sky. Beatrix Potter gave up writing children's stories to work amongst men like him. You could not imagine John Roper wearing any other clothes standing in any other place. He and it are one.

They say that once you go north you never go south again. Amongst the mountains and lakes, the sea and rolling pasture, is freedom and space – yet not too free and not too wide to be alienating. Like the sheep who eat almost anything, the gardener gardens almost anywhere, on scree and up mountainsides – in difficulty only when exposed along the north coast. It accounts for the variety of gardens in this book, each garden unlike the rest even if the same plants are used. The rhododendron, for example, is popular and ideally suited to this area but the ones you see in the grounds of Belle Isle, an island on Windermere, now sadly closed to the public, are a different visual treat from those seen deep in a woodland garden or silhouetted against a mountain.

These gardens are united as inspired personal visions we can tangibly admire. But there are those with visions who have sacrificed their gardens in order to enrich ours. One grows alpines on an exposed part of the Pennines and another grows cottage garden plants in Melkinthorpe, equally remote. These are plants we can buy knowing they won't promptly die of shock or live short, miserable lives in our climate. Someone who has not only dedicated his garden but his whole life to the great delight of primula lovers is Jared Sinclair. In spartan and often

JARED SINCLAIR

PEONIES AND LUPINS IN GREYSTOKE FOR EVERYONE; BELLE ISLE, WINDERMERE,
IN MAY; GARDENING IN A PAVEMENT CREVICE, GREYSTOKE;
A VISION OF SATURATED COLOUR NEAR BASSENTHWAITE

gruelling conditions he has carried the torch for Florence Bellis, who developed the Barnhaven primulas in Oregon. He is an unsung hero, having refused all offers of stardom on television, but our spring gardens would look a lot poorer without him.

This book would also look rather different were it not for the resilience of the owners of our 'stately homes' who stuck by them during the difficult post-war years and then went on to restore and reinspire gardens that would otherwise have disappeared. It is not easy to relinquish your privacy but it is characteristic of the British to rise to a challenge and turn it into a triumph. We see this in the work of the National Park and Trust and the private trusts that preserve the homes and gardens of Wordsworth and Ruskin.

The weather, however, protects the Lake District as effectively as the National Trust from a lethal dose of admirers, as a wet paradise is generally considered to be less alluring than a hot one. But the rain leaves the landscape deep in saturated colour and sunshine and cloud produce a kaleidoscopic interplay of light and shadow. Photographing Cumbria is a joy but gardening in this climate has all the makings of high anxiety. Step outside into brilliant sun and be greeted by cold lashing rain. Run back to climb into cagoule and wellies and suddenly it's summer. Fierce gales, horizontal rain, one good summer in ten makes a philosopher of you. Living here is a question of coping with extremes. It is extremely beautiful but also extremely wet and always unpredictable. Rough justice perhaps for living under the rainbow in the most visually exciting place in England. We get fed up and wonder why we live here, says Molly Birkett, and then we get one glorious day and we know.

Gardens are about people and people in the north are not as others are. Distance lends enchantment. Rain makes one eccentric. Original minds think original thoughts which create original gardens. The dreams we dream are tempered by an ill-tempered climate and an imposing landscape no one can ignore. We have to come to terms with nature. Our dreams have to be redreamt, our gardens rethought, but the dream is no less wonderful for all that.

Vivian R.

Dreaming the Dream

Isel Hall
Cockermouth

Mary Burkett

What can you say about one of the most popular and unique women in Cumbria who was as extraordinary when she lived in a 'wigwam' as she is now in the grandeur of Isel Hall, drove 18,000 miles in a Land Rover to explore Persia (now Iran), brought a praying mantis back from Perpignan to keep as a pet, and knows every eccentric, artistic, aristocratic or philanthropic person in Cumbria?

Mary Burkett grew up in Northumberland wanting to be a spy, detective and journalist, but became a teacher instead because her father advised her to, first in Warwickshire and then in the Lake District where she taught art and craft at the Charlotte Mason College in Ambleside. She then joined the fledgling Abbot Hall Art Gallery in Kendal, where she was paid 'a penny a week', and taught on the side to subsidize her work there. In 1966 she was made Director with one building and five staff and in 1973 it won the first Museum of the Year Award in England. She was given an OBE and 'retired', leaving five buildings and thirty-five staff. She then went around the world.

Her homes have always been interesting. Offered a flat at Abbot Hall, she turned it down because she preferred to use the space for exhibitions. Her boss, Peter Scott, dynamic chairman and founder of Abbot Hall and the Brewery Arts Centre, sold her a piece of land overlooking Lake Windermere and, being a true philanthropist, lent her the money to buy it. Soon afterwards she saw an advertisement in the paper for a Scandinavian A-frame house kit and promptly bought it. She named her home 'Demavend' after the highest mountain in Iran which apparently resembles a Norwegian A-frame house, and there she lived happily amongst the wild birds until someone she met at a strawberry party left her the house of the century.

Mrs Margaret Austen-Leigh was the childless widow of Jane Austen's great-nephew. She and Mary Burkett became great friends and, on her death, left Isel Hall to Mary, where she is now restoring the gardens.

Mary Burkett has sat on international committees, national committees, regional committees but, according to her, none so extraordinary and passionate as her local parish council. She's Chairman of the Appeal Committee for the Cumbria Wildlife Trust where she achieves the small miracle of pleasing everyone and still accomplishing a great deal. She is also currently involved in creating a museum in the now depressed West Cumbrian town of Maryport to give its residents 'a focus of their past' by housing the most fantastic collection of Roman altars and artefacts collected over 300 years by the Senhouse family, cousins to the Austen-Leighs.

But these are only wide circles around the core of her work, which has been to bring Cumbria's painting heritage out of the cellars where it often lay covered in soil. She is concentrating on seventeenth- and eighteenth-century portrait painters: 'These god-forsaken artists who sweated it out in the seventeenth and eighteenth centuries – why should they be forgotten?' She has taught Sir Roy Strong about John Bracken and has published books about William Green and Christopher Steele. She put together the first exhibition of James Blacklock, whom John Ruskin said was the 'only person who

OLD APPLE TREES IN THE SUNKEN GARDEN IN MAY

could paint the greens of the Lake District', and whom Turner called 'Britain's best watercolourist'.

In between leading tours to Turkey and restoring Isel Hall, Mary has been awarded a Leverhulme Fellowship to catalogue and photograph 2,000 Cumbrian portraits spanning four centuries in over eighty houses, all of which she has had to find herself. So the little girl who wanted to become a detective has become one after all.

'Earliest memories stick hard. One of my first is of sitting in a woodland glade amongst tall spring bracken fronds which were way above my head. The strong smell of their fresh tips when pressed between finger and thumb still takes me back instantly to that time, in the insistent way smells and sounds have of evoking the past. By the time I was eight, I had a passion for birds, woods, wild animals, nature and flowers. Although my love of cultivated gardens was still to be roused, wild gardens – nature's gardens – had already begun to excite me. In the intervening years I have had tiny gardens as small as 2 feet by 3 feet, and then the lovely little wild garden at Demavend, one-third of an acre, where tame robins, squirrels, blackbirds and I shared a little paradise of oaks, bluebells and Scotch pines. Living, as I did, in a tiny, tent-like house in the midst of them, they accepted me as part of their world. At Demavend, wild strawberries, violets and heartsease grew in the gravel path. Two azaleas, several rhododendrons and a birch surrounded me and I found the real solace of a garden. Living in a private world of my own, alongside flowers and birds, seemed like a dream but never did I dream of the paradise garden I was to inherit at Isel Hall.

'When I thought I ought to retire as Director of Abbot Hall, I felt I would not have enough to do so I lined up all sorts of projects and threw myself into committee work. My fears of idleness were groundless as, in August 1986, a dear friend and distant relative, Mrs Margaret Austen-Leigh, sadly died and left me Isel Hall and all its land and garden. On the many visits to her, I'd grown to love its beauty. Standing on a limestone bank high above a curve of the Derwent river, Isel Hall and its fourteenth-century pele tower have stood for centuries. Formerly the dower house of Brayton Hall (which was burnt to the ground in the 1920s), Isel has been first a Norman stronghold, then an Elizabethan manor house and in the sixteenth century it came into the hands of the Lawson family. The estates used to stretch south to the shores of Bassenthwaite Lake, north to Aspatria and west to the coast, but now there are just the fields and river banks immediately round the house as well as some woodland, a forest in the charge of the Forestry Commission, and one farm twenty miles away.

'Seen from any angle, there is magic in Isel Hall's setting which stirs the stoniest heart. The same feeling is roused inside the house where the old walls embrace you, despite the fact that they embrace quite a lot of water too, which is a problem that must

JUNE POPPIES OVERLOOKING THE DERWENT

be tackled. When a splendid hart's tongue fern grows three floors down in the pele tower, water must be getting in somewhere!

'But the garden now, as I sit out on the wide terrace facing south, is almost beyond verbal description. Above the river bank is an outer terrace, now ablaze with bright red poppies and marguerites dancing like white stars amongst them. Then there is a wide lawn running the length of the house. I have decided to leave the last fifty yards as a meadow. In spring it is carpeted with daffodils and in summer it is a mass of wild flowers, golden grasses, orchids, buttercups and speedwell.

'On the next terrace along the south wall of the house is a sandstone pavement and then formal beds. When I first saw these in the early 1960s they were full of roses, and there was a 'strawberry party' being held on the terrace. By the time I inherited, however, the roses had been attacked by deer and rabbits. Margaret Austen-Leigh loved animals and latterly enjoyed watching rabbits playing on the lawn, moles digging it up and deer creeping on to the terrace. I hope she will forgive me for discouraging all three from the top two layers of the garden.

'How was I, as an inexperienced gardener, to tackle these ten formal beds? To my rescue came a dear friend, Cornish Torbock, who offered to take charge of them. He decreed, "As far as possible they'll be work free, rabbit free, and not too tall – the sort of plants that will suit their setting." We chose plants such as dwarf lavender, lambs' ears, pink cranesbill, ladies' mantle, *Lysimachia cilesta* as edging plants, and each bed has a centre-piece such as a standard rose or fuchsia and regale lilies. The

MARY IN HER MONET GARDEN

spaces in between are filled with bedding material, such as tobacco plants. Against the house there are tulips and some lovely nerines as well as wisteria and a superb climbing rose, 'Maigold', which cascade around the door with exotic mixed scents.

'To the north of the house is a huge sunken garden – that will take time and thought to restore. Eventually, I hope that man and nature will come to an understanding and I'll return it to its former glory.

'As my life has been mainly concerned with the arts, I have developed favourite periods of flower and garden paintings. Artists such as Redon, Monet, Manet and Van Gogh seem to me to encapsulate the essence of flower painting. By their very nature, flowers are transient and, to me, the best method of depicting them is in the magnificent way created by the Impressionists. The water-lilies at Giverney, Van Gogh's sunflowers, and the poppies and meadows of Manet and Monet have just enough detail to identify the species and yet there is this wonderful free sense of wind playing on bending stems and light catching the brilliant petals. Here, at Isel, I have only to walk through the river terrace to be in a glorious Monet painting with rich, red poppies, marguerites and tall grasses waving in the breeze and glinting in the sunlight.

'Birds are always part of a garden. The swallows at Isel are still fairly numerous and goldcrests, greenfinches, warblers, robins and wrens nest in profusion. Every shed, nook and cranny now has a nest in it. Starlings are in the chimneys, together with jackdaws. Curlew float in front of red poppies while making the gurgling call so evocative of summer. In eastern Turkey there is a saying about Lake Van: "Van in this life, Paradise in the next" – I could happily substitute the word "Isel".'

R U S L A N D   H A L L
R U S L A N D

---

*J u l i a   P e i f f e r
W a t e n p h u l*

'Juju,' people said to me, 'is larger than life.' And this is true. She has a largesse of warmth, generosity, exuberance and her infectious laughter lights up all of Rusland Hall. Were she not married to the sensitive yet ever-practical Alexander, whom she always refers to modestly as 'the King', heaven knows where her flights of fancy and fantasy would take her. But however dear her husband is to her, don't be fooled into believing he is her greatest love for there is another gentleman involved, a certain Mr Bentley. And although some may shudder at the sound of him for he wheezes and snores, I lost my head over him the first time I saw his wonderful face as he pattered out of his front door to greet me with a toothy smile. He's only been known to bark once when, at 3 a.m., the Rusland Hall roof fell in. I expect this is a sign of good breeding as Mr Bentley is an English bulldog with exquisite manners.

Landscaped in the manner of Capability Brown with a view to moon over, Julia's garden is, in a sense, everywhere you look but the borders disappeared years ago, crushed under an advancing thicket of yew and rhododendron. So, for the moment, Mr Bentley moves about the garden in the guise of an ornamental statue, while the white peacocks are flowers of a surrealist kind.

The house is being restored, the garden cleared and redesigned to make way for flowers that are 'big and happy and full of laughter, like peonies and old roses. Not grim ones like irises, gladioli and some species of lilies.' There will be a fairy wood where Julia will put stone toadstool seats and stick cut-outs of deer, badgers and other wild animals which never stand still enough for her to sit and enjoy them. She wants to be reminded that they're out there somewhere. 'They'll amuse me and they'll amuse the fairies,' she says. 'What fairies?'

JULIA LOVES MR BENTLEY

Looking towards 'The Rusland Beeches'

I ask. 'Why, the elves and fairies that live on the ivy floor of the wood which is soft and marvellous. Of course, they're there, it's just that I've been too busy to see them yet.' Julia has enough yew to ward off witches and other evil spirits and she's concentrating on planting trees such as a Wellingtonia, hemlock, rowan and blossoming trees which 'the King' loves. In a huge beech tree she is building a treehouse for her eleven-year-old son, Charles, which you reach via a twisted spiral staircase around the trunk. In the treehouse will be a mattress and a pair of binoculars to observe the comings and goings of badger, deer and foxes. To come down, Charles will just have to swing on a rope.

'There have been two occasions in my life when I have experienced love at first sight. The first was meeting the man who was to become my wonderful husband, and the second time was driving through a beech wood, rounding a corner and seeing Rusland Hall standing in front of us, looking down her valley imperiously, with a halo of shimmering larches around her. Many, many years have passed since anyone had shown this old house any love or kindness. She was a Dowager in a tattered frock from another age.

'The garden was a wilderness of rare and ancient trees, uncomfortably embracing commonplace leylandii and laurels. Rhododendrons, like full-bosomed women dressed in afternoon tea frocks, made a wonderful display of loud and triumphant colour. Syca-more trees, grown tall and strong after their first hurried flight, had rooted themselves

THE PEACOCK 'GOD' ON THE LAWN

without thought or consideration for our views. They had quick and painless deaths, opening up a spectacular view of the nearby hillside speckled with sheep. Some of their roots are still buried deeply under the stony soil, with the nosy and ever-present laurels pushing their blowsy way forward. The laurels were also cut down in their prime but remain unwilling to relinquish their hold on this magical place. I am forever grateful that my husband has an artist's fine eye for beauty and a great ability to see how the garden can be created to give pleasure to all who visit her.

'We inherited several peacocks which, by their very presence, make the planting of small, flowering plants impossible as they find these a delicacy and can destroy many of them for lunch! Peacocks are beautiful birds and I would rather have a naked garden than part with our friends. Each one is named and has his or her own personality. During the months of April and May they are at their loudest, holding long conversations with one another in their ancient voices which can be heard in the furthest badger's set. Their bedroom is an enormous cedar tree. At dusk they assemble under their tree and fly up, each in turn. Onwards and upwards, a floor at a time, until they reach the safety of their precarious penthouse branch with views for many miles around. With the first light of a new day their small, powerful eyes open wide – a quick glance upwards – no buzzards; a glance downwards – no foxes – no danger. Time for an elegant gliding descent as breakfast awaits.

'When we first arrived, the garden had been neglected for years and we spent many hard hours uncovering the beauty that lay buried. One of our finds was a Victorian covered walk where the ladies would have strolled to take the air while remaining fashionably pale. We have planted many new trees: some strong, young oaks and also flowering trees which, when covered in their delicate lace blossom, look like young debutantes ready for their first dance. The beautiful beech tree with long, spreading arms provides shelter for the wild daffodils and my son and a friend gathered their courage and once slept in a tent under her branches. They lay trembling at the deep, gutteral sound of the deer calling to one another in the valley. To see five or six deer grazing in lush grass and wild anemones is a wonderful sight.

'As the end of the day approaches, the sheep quieten on the hillside and the air becomes still, as we wait expectantly for the moon and first stars to appear. It is at this peaceful time that my husband and I sit very still, leaning our tired backs against the silent strength of a large tree, listening to the sounds of the earth and the sky at the end of another perfect day. Our lives are rushing past us. We are so busy with our Rusland love affair: we will create something magical while we are here but a lifetime is too short to create a garden. We hope that our son, who loves Rusland as much as we do, will continue the creation of this piece of paradise for all to enjoy.'

C R A G   C O T T A G E
R O S T H W A I T E

S u e   F i s h e r

Sue Fisher is Cumbrian born and bred: she was born in Bassenthwaite village at the end of Bassenthwaite Lake and now lives at the end of Derwentwater, the next lake along.

She married a Fisher of Keswick, a colourful family of artists, potters and sculptors. Her father-in-law, Richard, trained as a painter and woodcarver at the Keswick Industrial Arts School founded by Canon Rawnsley and John Ruskin. Richard's twin brother, George Fisher, started the first mountaineering shop in the country which has become a national institution. He also led our Mountain Rescue Team for many years.

Sue Fisher and her husband, Allan, run a shop selling high-quality handmade furniture and crafts and Sue is one of the most amusing and droll people in Keswick. Her interest in gardening was inspired by her mother and by desperation at the state of the garden when she first moved to Crag Cottage. Gardening on a rocky outcrop requires a perverse will and once she had started she was, of course, hooked. In her years there she has turned it from a bare rock face into a unique garden with great style, finding out by trial and error which plants could survive the hostile environment. She writes:

'When we bought Crag Cottage thirteen years ago, the garden hadn't been touched for years. The only survivors of any previous garden were *Hypericum* (St John's wort) and *Saxifraga* (London Pride). The latter is essential as I plant it in front of new plants on the crag to hold back the ever elusive soil.

'The crag emerges about half-way across the garden and rises in stages to approximately forty feet. Apparently, young climbers used to 'rope-on' here to practise and improve their skills, skills I should possibly have tried to master to improve my chances when negotiating my 'rock garden'.

'Most of my first efforts at planting were duly consumed by herbivorous Herdwick sheep which can eat their way into any gap or, seemingly, over any wall. A cow also dropped in from the crag on one occasion; none the worse for its journey, it found its feet, bellowed and nonchalantly walked away. Our boundaries have now taken on a Fort Knot appearance and we are troubled no more by unwelcome visitors.

'Our garden problems now lie within: we have two young sons who bear a closer relationship to mountain goats than to their parents and they bring their friends to play on our very exciting crag. At the end of the day my plants lie flattened and I have to explain to anxious parents that the bandages and plasters sported bravely by their dear little offspring are remnants of a very adventuresome day falling down my crag.'

SUSAN, GRAEME AND TEAL, THE DOG, CRAGFAST

B R A N T W O O D
C O N I S T O N

J o h n   R u s k i n ' s   G a r d e n

The story of John Ruskin's garden at Brantwood is a curious one, for John Ruskin, even by his own admission, was a very curious person. It is probably less of a 'garden' than any of the others in this book, partly because it has been left to its own devices for nearly ninety years but also because Ruskin hated forced flowers like 'nasty gloxinias and glaring fuchsias' and thought glasshouses, or hothouses as they were then called, practically immoral. So no formal parterre for him, only the wildness of the woods yielding hardy yet more delicate flowers. In these woods he fashioned a unique garden deploying the many talents, enthusiasms and peculiarities of this high priest of the Victorian era.

Ruskin's garden became so inextricably bound up with his work, moods, philosophies, interests, hopes and fears that, in many ways, Brantwood became the ultimate dream garden. In it he dreamt his dreams for a happier England, an England he saw depersonalized by the Industrial Revolution – its people alienated from their work and their land. In his own way, at Brantwood, he tried to show how this could be changed.

It was a philosophy he was committed to all his life and had its seeds sown many years before in the garden of his childhood home at Camberwell Green. His mother was an evangelical Christian with firm principles. Tutored at home, he grew up in a world of his own, and the garden was his world. It was a garden of fruiting trees but he was not allowed to pick any of the fruit, writing later that the only difference he perceived between this garden and the Garden of Eden was that in this one 'all the fruit was forbidden'. He was further alienated from it by the gardeners. If he swept and weeded, the gardeners would come and sweep and weed after him. If he became intrigued by an ant's nest it was brushed away for being untidy. Unable to become a participant he became an observer, obsessed with plants, not

RUSKIN'S HOUSE FRAMED BY AZALEAS
HE PLANTED HIMSELF

23

wanting to grow them but merely to stare at them, 'or into them. In no morbid curiosity but in admiring wonder, I pulled every flower to pieces until I knew all that could be seen of it with a child's eyes; and used to lay up little treasures of seeds, by way of pearls and beads, never with any thought of sowing them. . . I was extremely fond of digging holes, but that form of gardening was not allowed.' He was later to attribute his 'acute perception and deep feeling for the beauty of architecture and scenery abroad' which made him so famous to 'the well formed habit of narrowing myself to happiness within the four brick walls of our 50 by 100 yards of garden.'

The 'creation of the world', though, happened on the day his nurse took him to Friar's Crag on Derwentwater whilst the family were holidaying in the Lake District. There he felt 'intense joy, mingled with awe' as he looked through the hollows of mossy roots, over the crag and into the dark lake.

Perhaps because of his extraordinary sensitivity, Ruskin was particularly affected by his childhood. He lived with his parents until they both died, and then, when he was free, the Lake District called him back.

Ruskin bought Brantwood, his first home, at the age of 52 after a long illness during which he imagined he could only recover there. 'Brant' is a northern word for steep and the house came with fourteen acres of fellside woods and a fine view over Coniston Lake. 'Here I have rocks, streams, fresh air and for the first time in my life the rest of a purposed home . . . with hedges of wild roses, fern, honeysuckle, moss, real rock and heather, circling copse, a stream, and moorland on which the monks of Furness first tilled the soil and tended sheep . . . and a lovely field with nothing visible over the edge of its green waves but the lake and sunset.'

The little boy who was never allowed to dig in his garden now believed in digging of all sorts. 'I am at work in my own little garden among the hills, conscious of little more than the dust of the earth.' Together with the twelve gardeners he brought with him from the south, he threw all his energies into creating a network of woodland tracks all over the fellside. Some led to waterfalls, some to interesting rocks, others to fine viewpoints. He concentrated upon realizing the full potential of all the natural features of his garden. W. G. Collingwood, his secretary, called him the first true Lake District landscape gardener.

From his stream, Ruskin made a series of reservoirs with gates and sluices which, when opened, produced a roaring waterfall down the fell and past his front door. In nooks, crannies or bosses of rock he made gardens of wild flowers such as hyacinth and wood anemone, or moss and fern. For himself, he made a private, terraced garden bordered by a stone wall in the heart of the wood, a steep beck with rocky cascades, and wooden paling against which he grew espaliered apples. Near the beehive he planted cottage garden flowers such as pinks, campanula, sweet william and primroses in and amongst the strawberries and the gooseberry patch. His ivy bank was covered in periwinkle. He took wild flowers from the higher fells and transplanted them beside his streamlets, waterfalls and cascades. By the side of the house and down by the lake he planted a crooked path of orange and yellow *Azalea luteum* which still survives today, the only remains of his flower plantings. The many rhododendron hybrids he planted in the woodland have all now reverted to the purple *ponticum*.

Ruskin used his garden to carry out his ideas on social reform. He created an ice house so the poor could have access to cold compresses; he set up a trout farm to provide food; and he used his terraced reservoirs as an example from Italy on irrigation. But the most important experiment was his creation of a moorland garden, 500 feet up the fell with a marvellous view, to illustrate his theory of reclaiming wasted land. By terracing, draining and improving the soil, large areas of rank bog grass could be turned into productive land. Corn was planted but failed and was replaced by apple and cherry trees which did grow. His friend Susan Beever, who lived locally, gave him cranberries to plant in the soggy patch on this moor. He wrote to her afterwards, 'The whole household was out after breakfast today to the top of the moor to plant cranberries; and we

VIEW OF THE CONISTON FELLS OVER *AZALEA LUTEUM*

squeezed and splashed and spluttered in the boggiest places the lovely sunshine had left, till we found places squashy and squeezy enough to please the most particular and coolest of cranberry minds; and then each of us choosing a little special bed of bog, the tufts were deeply put in with every manner of tacit benediction, such as might befit a bog and a berry.'

It did not matter to him that planting large areas of British mountain ground with crops to feed the poor people of the world was economically naive. He hated commercialism and possessive wealth, measuring the wealth of a country only by its people's sense of self-worth. 'As long as there are hands unemployed and misemployed, a government such as mine would never be at a loss for labourers. If corn can be made to grow where juniper grew before, the benefit is a positive one, the expense only comparative.' He, however, was going broke and his original workforce of twelve gardeners dwindled to friends and students visiting from Oxford, where he was Slade Professor.

Using the talent he had developed as a child to so 'minutely see and so accurately reproduce', Ruskin delighted in studying and drawing his flowers, filling the margins of his diary with illustrations of them next to entries such as this: 'July 3 – sun on fells and cranberry blossom in my saucer ready to be drawn. Yesterday in breezy afternoon found them all on the hill sparkling like rubies.' Seascale was his favourite place to sketch the purple geraniums and dwarf roses on the dunes. He who hated the blast furnaces of Broughton in Furness and blamed them for the black 'plague cloud' and most of the bad weather, was actually sitting on the future site of Sellafield.

Ruskin also wanted to recreate tableaux of Italy and France in his gladed garden. It was common practice at the time to cut coppices of oak and hazel for charcoal burning and turning bobbins. But Ruskin let the trees in his coppice grow into slender willowy stems so that the mountains and lake behind might seem more veiled and tantalizing, like the background to the high altars in the paintings of Botticelli. The moorland garden wasn't fenced off because he had a vision of the moor as 'a para-

'NABOTH'S VINEYARD', CONISTON

dise of terraces like the top of the purgatorial Mount in Dante'. Even the tennis lawn he created for the 'enjoyment of his younger guests' was designed in the style of a 'purist's painter glade'.

Ruskin was happiest in the wooded glade that was his garden. 'Anemone and primrose totally divine

now in my woods – primroses on my own rocks, beyond dream beautiful.' After a morning's writing he would pick up his gloves and billhook, which always lay on the hall table, to do an hour's chopping to keep his coppice mysterious and his mind and body healthy. Sadly, the only work of his he considered of any importance – his writings on social reform – were completely ignored by the public and he sunk into periods of profound melancholia, haunted by thoughts of his own death and comparing it to the death of every flower.

His physical and financial limitations restricted his work on the garden, which gradually degenerated. W. G. Collingwood described his last years thus: 'The hills were a comfort to him, the flowers of his garden and moor were a joy. During the last decade when he wandered about his small domain like the ghost of his former self, no one could carry on his work. The paths he made and tended gradually became overgrown, the rocky watercourses were choked with stones, his private plot filled with weeds for he could no longer dig it.' Towards the end when he couldn't move or speak, or even recognize anyone around him, Canon Rawnsley remembers a bouquet of wild flowers being placed before him. His eyes lit up and fastened on them with 'childlike wonder' staring with all the absorption of a 'long, steady carpet-gazer'.

Now, nearly ninety years after Ruskin's death, his garden is being restored by Bruce Hanson, the director of Brantwood. Bruce Hanson wanted to restore the garden but he had to find it first. He knew what was supposed to be there, but where? I spent a day with him, scrabbling about the partially restored network of paths like Indiana Jones in search of the lost city. Gradually, the garden was revealed to me, like pentimento, with the barest outline showing through, nature having almost effaced all traces by knitting plants together to form an impenetrable jungle. There are no surviving plans that anyone knows of and trying to draw a map based on the entries in Ruskin's diaries is like solving an anagram, for example, 'Went in, found tea wasn't till seven – went out again – up to the little garden in the twilight across the bridge, down to terrace of great garden – to and fro there a little. Down to the gate and up again – after standing at the gate (Wishing gate) and saying the Lord's Prayer, went up then into my field – to and fro there, thinking of my father.'

Bruce Hanson has managed to unravel the garden. He discovered the clues lay not only in the diaries but in the paths. Every time the hint of a path was uncovered he would follow it to see where it led. Then, along the way, he might find a couple of steps or another path leading to something else and so it went, so that now, expertly guided by Bruce, you too will be able to see the remains of the lost garden of Ruskin.

H U T T O N - I N - T H E -
F O R E S T , P E N R I T H

*R i c h a r d a n d
C r e s s i d a V a n e*

It has been said that it is much more exciting to explore a garden oneself than to be shown around it. This must be equally true of the discovery of the garden itself and is part of the special mystique that Hutton-in-the-Forest holds for me.

I was returning home one day by way of an unfamiliar route when a sign for 'Hutton-in-the-Forest' suddenly materialized after a sharp bend in the road. It was nearly dusk, and I looked forward to exploring the garden at that magical hour. The air was utterly still, the atmosphere close. Hoping I wasn't about to intrude into a private garden, I hesitantly unfastened the latch on the small gate and pushed through the secret door.

As I stepped out of the copse, wooden gates and the pele tower of a medieval castle rose before me under a thunderous black cloud. The fells and lakes of my other world seemed far away as I was drawn into this enchanted kingdom. Reality quickly intruded and, pelted with hail and rain, I ran for cover through the open door and began to read the information leaflets set out. The history of Hutton-in-the-Forest, part of the Royal Forest of Inglewood, was intriguing. Legend has it that the original manor house was the Green Knight's castle in one of the Arthurian tales, *Sir Gawain and the Green Knight*. It is known for certain that Edward I visited Hutton in 1292. The gardens of Hutton were first laid out in the seventeenth century and were later redesigned in the Victorian manner during the nineteenth century.

Once the rain had subsided, I ventured across the large courtyard to the terraces at the front of the house, which overlooked a low, woodland garden of what is now mainly *Rhododendron ponticum* – its grassy vista stretching to a glassy lake and cascade. On the banks of the terrace a group of centenarian yews stood clustered together like a group of garden party guests. I followed the terrace and yew hedges round the back of the house where an arch of yew led me into the square walled garden which was flanked by a *Rosa rugosa* walk and further protected by a circle of sentinel columnar yews. In the middle of the walled garden was a little cherub, marking the centre of the quadrangle.

Along the main border, dashing blue lupins escorted blowsy crinoline poppies.

ROSA RUGOSA HEDGE HIGHLIGHTED
AGAINST DRAMATIC SKY

These strong shapes and colours were striking against the brooding sky and turreted outline of the castle. I came across a weathered wooden bench under a yew hedge. Along the top was carved 'I Was New When Cressida Wed Richard'. I wondered, as I left the gardens, who Richard and Cressida were and what had become of them, for I had still not met a single person there.

Richard and Cressida, it transpired later, had only been married a year. Richard Vane is the elder son of the present Lord Inglewood and has taken charge of Hutton-in-the-Forest. He is Eton- and Cambridge-educated, a qualified planning law barrister, a member of the North West Water Authority, sits on the Lake District Special Planning Board, is quickwitted, precise, articulate and only thirty-six. Leaving a well-paid job in London, he had chosen to return to Hutton in his mid-twenties. Taking on a stately home is like becoming a parent to Peter Pan: the responsibilities are enormous and with you always. But Richard is philosophical about it: 'You've got to take a view of what you want to do with your life, haven't you? Much better to enjoy what you're doing and make a go of it, whatever that may be, rather than fret about what might have been.'

'Other people's gardens aren't interesting until you have your own,' he says. Yet his garden isn't really just his creation as it's packed with plants grown over the last 200

years. As a member of the Planning Board, he is used
to making aesthetic decisions about other people's
proposals but in his own garden he is hesitant about
change. 'If, for instance, you look down from the terrace towards the cascade there are one or two fine
trees that block out some really rather splendid
views of the lake beyond. Now what do you do? It
seems heresy to chop the trees down but it would
perhaps be a bit nicer if you did and you've got to
make those sorts of value judgements which are a bit
difficult at the time. You inherit an eighteenth-
century walled garden which you would like to restore and maintain properly but you have only one
gardener, not the necessary six, so you are con-
strained by a framework of compromise.'

CRESSIDA, RICHARD AND MIRANDA

Richard Vane's greatest passion is trees. The best thing he can remember about
the garden from his childhood is planting the saplings that are now almost fully grown
trees. 'When you've got a garden like this you can play around with real trees when
most people play around with miniatures. You can scatter conifers across this garden
in the way most people have to scatter bonsai. It's a great privilege to be able to do
it on a big scale. The fact that I won't see them in their full glory doesn't matter
somehow.'

When Richard married Cressida Pemberton-Pigott he led the garden into its ren-
aissance. Cressida is primarily a landscape and garden photographer, best known for
her work in *The Englishwoman's Garden* and, most recently, for *Beatrix Potter's Lakeland*.
Although she lived in London for the last twenty years, she was brought up at Fawe
Park on Derwentwater. Her London garden was a vibrant patch in Brixton, filled with
camellias, roses ('not the ones that are all stalks'), and peonies ('they're so extrava-
gant'). She was very happy there but left it for marriage and a very much grander garden set in a landscape she loves. She is elegant, reserved and softly spoken but her vision
of the garden's future is as clear as Richard's. 'One thinks that if you love gardens and
have been photographing them, you will understand why they are so successful. That
may be true but actually doing it yourself is a great challenge.'

Helping them to do that is the new gardener,' Ian Corri who trained at the Chelsea
Physic Garden, London, and later worked at Holker Hall in Cumbria. 'Everybody puts
his oar in here. So there are plants in the garden that mean something to each person.
Lord Inglewood likes flowers that mark the seasons and has the house filled with snow-

drops in March. Mr Vane likes lupins and Mrs Vane doesn't. Mrs Vane likes colour, forms of leaves and looks at the shape and performance of a plant. Mr Vane likes trees and has the basis for a good arboretum here. He likes pines and conifers and has better facilities for a pinetum which would be an interesting project as there is none in the north-west that stands out.' Ian Corri personally prefers rare forms of common plants such as verbascum, aquilegias and foxgloves. He has taken the advice of Mike Swift, head gardener at Lingholm Gardens, to plant things that will 'stop the public in their tracks. They haven't come all this way to see plants they grow at home.'

The stream which encircles the house and runs through the woodland garden and into the lake is one of the best features of the garden. Cressida is planning to plant primulas, polyanthus and 'other half-wild things' along its banks. She thinks the garden will begin to fulfil its potential in several years' time. At the front of the house she is planning a wildflower bank and she will turn the walled garden into a flower garden, perhaps with a knot garden and potager. From the moment a garden is begun it is rarely finished. Two hundred years after these gardens were first laid out, the owners are still making plans as if it were almost new.

THE *ROSA RUGOSA* WALK

T H E   O L D   S C H O O L
M U N G R I S D A L E

D o r o t h y   C h a l k

When I first saw Dorothy's garden filled with Wordsworth's 'silent overgrowings', it seemed like a corner of the secret garden had been left untouched. Sweet rocket and red poppies bloomed like flowers in a meadow. The shrub roses were still in bud and the apple trees, soft fruit and potatoes growing in an old water tank all flourished together amongst a canopy of weeds that stretched from the bottom of the garden to the top. It looked far wilder than the fell that rose behind the house which, being well tended by Lakeland's most compulsive gardeners – the ever-pruning sheep, looked positively municipal by comparison.

As I was admiring this rarest of gardens, a woman from the village came to post a letter in the box set inside the stone wall. I asked who lived here. 'Miss Chalk. She's very nice, but eccentric. Collects rubbish.' A fellow hoarder, I thought, knowing how things tend to get exaggerated in the Lake District. I photographed the garden from outside the gate and presently Miss Chalk came along. She smiled at me immediately. Shy, but obviously pleased, she opened the gate for me and released the garden. Then she disappeared up the garden path. Delighted at last to have found a wonderfully un-

tidy garden, as natural as a garden ever can be, I became absorbed in photographing the patterns of the poppies. When I had finished, I went up to the house where I saw rabbits in cages and Oscar the drake and his harem paddling about the fell. I knocked on the door and, as Dorothy let me in, I noticed another

DOROTHY'S 'SILENT OVERGROWINGS'

door to what must have been the old schoolroom which was full of literally thousands of books on shelves. What had been described to me earlier as rubbish was, in fact, books finding their way back to the schoolroom.

'This is where I do my entertaining,' said Dorothy as we squeezed into a kitchen the size of a closet and sat on our

32

respective stools, our knees practically touching. I asked her about her life. 'I'm a Lan-cashire lass,' she replied, born in Lytham St Annes where she spent a happy childhood. Her first job was teaching in Hull for one year then in a secondary school in the East End of London which she found a nightmare. She became ill with 'worry' and left before the end of the first term, as did six others who began with her. She started to work in a biscuit factory in Bermondsey, taking evening classes in statistics, and eventually gained the certificate of the Royal Statistical Society. She then worked at the BBC in overseas broadcasting but, after ten years in London, decided that it was 'ten years too long' so she subscribed to the *Cumberland and Westmorland Herald* to 'broaden her hori-zons' and see what was going on in an area she had known and loved from holidays spent there as a child.

She saw an advertisement for the old schoolhouse at Mungrisdale and made the owners an offer to which they responded, 'We were thinking of five times that.' Her widowed mother helped her out financially and they both moved in. Dorothy did supply teaching and her mother took on the post office. Together they ran the post office for nearly twenty years until her mother died. Although Dorothy wanted to continue it, she told me that they hadn't been too organized and had 'lost things' and 'what the Post Office would tolerate in a dear old lady of eighty, they weren't prepared to put up with in a younger version.' So, Dorothy concluded to me, these were hard times.

She earns some money by selling her rabbits, which she first farmed for their pelts during the war. She had had a pet rabbit, a show champion. 'I've still got a pair of gloves, of which he is one,' she said wistfully. She gets eggs from her Indian Runners, a breed of ducks reputed to be the most nervous of all. They are a delightful bottleshape, with long necks and round bottoms like Jemima Puddleduck. They are intensely curious creatures but are hopeless as guards because they don't want to attract interest to themselves. Three of her ducks are sisters and always get broody together and lay eggs on the same nest.

None has been seduced by a certain long-tailed gentleman with sandy whiskers but that's partly because they are shut in at dusk and locked in the garden in spring when the vixens are feeding their young. While the ducks are in the garden they eat any slugs that may be overwintering there. But, as the weed jungle begins to rise ever higher, the ducks find it claustrophobic and return to the fell.

Dorothy describes her garden as 'a conservation area in the spring which turns into a disaster area by August'. And, although she agrees that a weed is only a plant growing in the wrong place – a view shared by Wordsworth – she does admit to a few too many. Yet ten-foot nettles keep people away from her fruit netting. She did not

IMPRESSIONISTIC POPPIES AND SWEET ROCKET

plant the goosegrass deliberately but one year it happened to grow over her redcurrants and raspberries and every year since then they've remained untouched by the birds. But life is full of ironies. Recently, she told me she'd been peeling away the goosegrass and had filled a bowlful of glorious raspberries which she'd set down in order to pull out a few nettles and reach another patch when, suddenly, there was a huge quack and a great flapping of wings and the ducks flew down the path to land right in the middle of her bowl of raspberries. The sheep had just wandered back on to the fell, freshly shorn and dyed from woolly grey to smooth, flaming red, and had frightened these nervous little ducks senseless. So, in the end, nobody got the raspberries, except the slugs.

In the summer of 1976 when there was drought and water rationing all over England and nobody could grow blackcurrants, Dorothy thought hers would be dead too, but after she'd trampled her way to them, she found that the high weeds had blocked the drying winds and the shorter weeds had protected the roots of the black-currant bushes from the sun. The soil had retained the moisture and she was the only person in Cumbria that summer with a bumper crop.

'I do enjoy pushing my way through undergrowth and seeing things move. One does need a conservation area: I never do any autumn clearing and I haven't done any in early May for two years!' Her favourite flowers are those which like to grow in her garden.

34

C O O M B E C O T T A G E
B O R R O W D A L E

V i v i a n R u s s e l l

I was told some time ago that you should plan your garden as if you're going to live for ever and look after it as if you're going to die tomorrow. This didn't cut any ice with my spouse who, after a stroll around Hillier's Arboretum, ordered a weeping alder tree like the one he nostalgically remembered playing under as a child. When the 'tree' arrived, it had us all weeping. A garden gnome would have towered over it and it seems to grow only sideways. Maybe our children will sit under it when they are aged parents but my sixty-year-old husband never will. He was most indignant.

So, for Ken I plant for the present, and for my children I plant a garden of wonderful scents as that is what they will remember when they are grown up: jasmine, honeysuckle, old roses, pinks, viburnums, catmint and *phuopsis* which reminds me of the skunks of Connecticut – and inside our small conservatory, lemon and jasmines collected on my travels, *Rhododendron 'Fragrantissimum'*, trumpet lilies and a wonderful, blowsy, pink rose called 'Columbian Climber' which does not appear in any catalogue but which I obtained from Lingholm Gardens across the lake. I brought this orphaned beauty to Peter Beales's rose nursery for adoption so you must pester him for it. My children are quite blasé about my efforts but are bound to catch the odd whiff of heaven as they forage for lost toys. And when they do grow up they'll probably remember with great affection some prickly weed I tossed without a second thought on the compost heap. For myself, I plant for the future. In and amongst the kaleidoscope of muted pinks, reds and mauves of the self-seed-

MOLLY SQUEEZED INTO A NOW
IMPENETRABLE PATH

ing poppies which I love the best, I have planted in our Hampshire garden rare magnolias, davidias (the pocket-handkerchief tree), eucryphias and hoherias because I love white flowering trees. In our Cumbrian garden, which is very small, I have planted old-fashioned plants for

Ken, and box and yew for my old age. They don't look very attractive at present but no one has any idea of the garden I have in mind for the future, a garden very different from the one you see in the pictures: a topiary of pudding trees and peacocks.

It has taken me ten years to arrive at the very simple solution to our capricious climate and one which someone who had lived here before me must have arrived at because I have been told this garden used to be full of topiary pieces. As I write this, we had a drought in June and more rain in July than in 106 years, and we are already the wettest place in Britain. There are twenty-two kinds of rain listed in the Thesaurus and sometimes we get them all at once. Just when the lupins are looking nice we have what Molly Birkett calls 'our lupin weather' which is a lovely way of describing torrential rain chased by gale force winds. I remember one blustery summer when I was quite new to gardening and still under the illusion that love conquers all. I had planted a wondrous English garden of tall campanulas, delphiniums, lupins, lychnis and verbascum but by the end of the summer every plant in the garden was either tied to a stake or moored to its stronger neighbour. And for a while after that when people used to compliment me on the garden asking what they should grow up here I'd say stick to heather and gorse and walk away.

The more I looked at our topiary bird who has quietly been sitting there for a hundred years impervious to any weather, looking wonderful in any season, requiring only the occasional trim and to whom the birds fly in spring to make their nest, who doesn't need to be sprayed or slug proofed, dead headed or divided, the more obvious became what should have been obvious from the start. I had been greatly taken with Marjorie Fish's 'pudding trees' in her garden and, since conifers don't texturally fit into this garden, I thought we would have them in box. So I've planted *Box pyramidalis* and surreptitiously installed several young yews and in my mind's eye I see this dream-child years from now with judiciously placed pudding trees and topiary birds, underplanted with the simplest of flowers – marguerites, poppies, dwarf lupins, columbines, mallow, tulips, burnet and China roses, sweet williams – and maybe globe artichokes and purpley Brussels sprouts! In winter I will have a garden of soft green sculpture which would be magical in the frost and snow, and in the summer an Alice in Wonderland atmosphere.

JULY ROSES BEFORE THE DELUGE

THIS LABURNUM PRODUCED ONLY THREE RACEMES
THE FOLLOWING YEAR!

Since most of our garden can be taken in at a glance from the road it has to register an instant cohesive impression, rather like looking at a photograph or painting. Every part of it has to work at once with all the other parts. It isn't a garden of many surprises. It's got two. A front and a back. The back is cobblestoned, like a cloister, and this I call my Garden of Hints. It's white with blushes of primrose or pink and contains many species roses, all the astrantias, the poppy 'Cedric Morris', white foxgloves and lilies, hostas, *choisya*, Solomon's seal, white shrubs, grey foliage plants and a great laburnum which contributes a blast of yellow for a few weeks before returning it to its subtleties. The year after I renamed this corner 'The Garden of Hints' the laburnum produced only three racemes. Many people pass by our front gate, often pausing to scrutinize the wild and weedy offerings on display, now rather less replete with poppies, foxgloves, hollyhocks and cranesbill than before. I live next to a farm whose woolly inmates often escape to come to me for a gourmet meal but luckily species roses aren't on the menu.

I think the best gardens are the impressionistic gardens – where everything is reflected in everything else. Ruskin once said that 'repetition is the essence of design' and you only have to look at the most perfect garden of all, a wildflower meadow, to know that this is true.

TOPIARY YEW RULES THE ROOST

S C A R T H W A I T E
G R A N G E - I N -
B O R R O W D A L E

N a n   H i c k s

Nan and Sam Hicks' garden was featured in the *Sunday Express* when it won the Garden of the Year competition but I had never heard of it. One of the reasons I was the last person to know I was living one mile away from the greatest revelation of my life was that Nan and Sam Hicks, although vitally involved in the community, are very self-effacing people.

Nan Hicks is a former nursing sister, governor of the Borrowdale School, painter, embroiderer and superb gardener. She was recruited by the Marie Curie Foundation and nurses cancer patients in their homes, often 'walking the last few miles of their lives with them'. 'It's very fulfilling – sad but, in a funny sort of way, there's joy in it too. It's a great privilege.' Her work can be painful and exhausting, but when she gets home she goes into the garden and becomes absorbed in that. She and Sam have been at Scarthwaite for thirty years and have created a lovely garden with a stupendous backdrop.

'If you are of the Parks Department School of gardening you will be very disappointed with my garden. There are no strictly regimented carpet beds or carefully manicured lawns but, if you think as I do, you could well be pleased. The garden is very small, brimful of plants growing in what could be described as gay abandon. Surrounded as it is by beautiful wild and rugged crags and mountains, a formal garden would be totally out of place. The stone of the house was quarried from local rock – beautiful blue-green blocks of Honister slate – so that it too appears to be part of the scenery. The environment dictated the style. A scheme was devised of informal planting with the boundaries to the south and west, which border the open countryside, appearing to merge with the landscape beyond. The scenery has been borrowed from outside, giving the impression of being part of the garden. This required as careful planning as any formally-defined garden. I hope a sense of mystery prevails, indicating an element of controlled wildness. It is, in fact, organized chaos.

'Overlying everything is a sense of greenness. Textures, plant shapes and forms play as important a part in the design as colour. Because the garden is so small and overplanted, trees and shrubs have to be ruthlessly pruned and cut back, but in such a

manner as to appear natural. The two privet boundaries with my neighbours are seen from the road and provide the only concessions to formality as I try to keep them fairly groomed. This is a form of deceit as it gives the passer-by the idea that the gardener is in control. There is no lawn, only a broad grass path

NAN HICKS; (PREVIOUS PAGE)
RHODODENDRON 'SAPPHO'
....

wandering through the borders, and this too I try to keep looking neat. I feel that if these two elements of the whole are fairly tidy they will pull together what would otherwise be a very messy plot.

'Alongside British native plants grow exotics from many corners of the world and much thought has been put into making these foreigners feel at home in their alien environment. It pleases me when visitors tell me that they have wandered around my garden several times and that on each occasion have discovered something they had missed previously. Certainly, over the seasons there are eyecatchers, as when a particular clematis blooms, a favourite rhododendron flowers, or when the Lenten lilies are a blaze of yellow. But when each has had its moment of glory, it recedes and allows another to take the stage.

'The soil is very poor and stony and is impossible to dig with a spade. I use a potato fork to cultivate what earth there is. Perhaps I grumble overmuch about the gravel and stones. What the soil lacks in humus it makes up for in drainage. But for this, many of my plants would never survive the winter. The rainfull is around ninety inches *per annum* but, even with all that rain, there are occasions in summer when I need to water and carry many bucketfuls to thirsty hydrangeas. Planting is close and thick, leaving little room for weeds. Such weeds as there are are there by invitation – speedwells in the grass by the washing line, and celandines and forget-me-nots near by, lady's smock and sweet woodruff in the hedge bottoms with gowans, foxgloves and male ferns by the wall.

'I once tried to catalogue all my plants and was defeated by the task. I think the last count of clematis alone came to something like seventy but I am not sure how many there really are as, from time to time, the odd one succumbs to clematis wilt and is struck off the register, only to reappear as if resurrected in another season.

'Each year is different. The garden evolves and changes as time goes by. Some plants give up the struggle to grow in alien surroundings. Others feel truly at home, seed and, in turn, produce new life the following year. So the pattern changes just as the image in a kaleidoscope alters but the overall beauty is the same and I love it.'

B E T H A V E N
G R A S M E R E

J o h n   I n g h a m

When I arrived to interview John Ingham on the wildest, wettest afternoon of the winter, there were three inches of rain rushing down his garden path. It had rained all day and every other day that month save one. An irrepressible hobbyist, John had just finished an intricate 1,500-piece jigsaw on Twenty Species of British Garden Birds. He knew them all by name, of course, just as he knows all about wildflowers, trees, plants and minerals – what they're called and where to find them – identifying each one as easily as the thousands of households he looked after during his forty years in Her Majesty's Royal Mail.

Tall and lanky, with infinitely long legs which stretch right across the sitting room, John is a man with plenty of ideas, opinions, and a unique turn of phrase.

Born in County Durham in 1917, he had come, as so many do, to the Lake District on school holidays, staying with friends whose Hawkshead house had a lovely garden of rose arches and a croquet lawn. Hawkshead is renowned for having schooled Wordsworth, but it didn't school John Ingham, even after he came one holiday, aged fifteen, and never went home again. In his own words, he just 'parped about' which is an old Cumbrian phrase for 'messing about'.

He builds a romantic picture of Hawkshead in those 'far off days. Ruined now, of course.' The village stream, Black Beck, was filled with trout, the surrounding fields with plover, and in the marshes amidst the rushes and reeds you could hear the snipe drumming away with their wings on a sum-

JOHN AND MRS GAIR'S SWEETBRIAR
....

mer's evening, and the odd curlew calling. Now there's a big sign up 'No Bathing or Paddling', the water is polluted with toilet paper from the campsite and the village is made up of 'cafés, bloomin' knick knack shops, and a great big car park'. The birds were frightened away long ago.

John joined the

Hawkshead sub post office at nineteen as Country Postman, doing nineteen and a half miles on the rural round and averaging sixty to seventy calls a day on foot and bicycle. However slippery the hilly roads, however fierce the storms, he never missed a day's work due to bad weather. He is at his most wistful when he says that now everybody at Hawkshead has become a stranger to him. 'I don't know anybody now – I don't know all these other people.' He certainly knew everybody then, all the old families, and he envied them their gardens.

As he opened Mrs Gair's garden gate, he would nip a piece off her sweetbriar and smell the leaves as he walked up the path to the house, its scent especially delicious in spring after an afternoon's rain. And he had his eye on Mr Metcalf's *Dicentra spectabilis* from the moment he saw those delicate, pink, heart-shaped lockets hanging fast on an arched stem in the bitterest of spring winds. 'One day I'll have one of them,' he would say to himself, the way other men look at fast cars.

Now, many years later, his spring garden is filled with Bleeding Heart and the sweet scent from the 8-foot sweetbriar by his front door which he grew from a cutting of Mrs Gair's rose. But in the 1930s, having his own garden seemed a long way off.

In 1948, bachelor life gave way to married life. His in-laws bought him and his wife Betty a 'town house' with a bit of ground. But it was ground made black by the soot of the chimneys and he felt like a fish out of water every minute of his time there, preferring to travel four miles over slippery or snowy roads on dark winter mornings than to live without a garden. 'I missed it so much.'

When he was made Postal Inspector in 1956 he moved back to Hawkshead. If anybody ever tells you people in the provinces don't get around, show them this!

In 1970, seven years before he retired, John bought a traditional stone cottage on a third of an acre on the very lower steppes of Heron Pike, in Grasmere. The garden was a jungle but, with the help of 'good handy lads from the Post Office', they soon cleared it. He and Betty decided to plant 'Old English roses all the way.' Why? 'Well, it's an old cottage, isn't it? I like smelling the roses, even if you do get a noseful of greenfly.'

Together they compiled a list of thirty-six including moss, gallica, rugosa (for the flowers all summer long) and musk and handed it to the local nursery who scoured England for them. John had good drainage provided by field drains from the fell and also dug in plenty of well-rotted compost into his acid soil. A friend from Hawkshead sowed a lawn for him.

In amongst the roses went meconopsis, campanulas, lychnis, verbascum, cranes-bills, polyanthus, tradescantia, lavender, delphiniums and lupins and, behind his greenhouse grows the Eighth Wonder of the World, now fifteen years old – a trillium with fifty blooms on it. John insists that his love of flowers and gardening is in the blood.

His mother's family were market gardeners for eighty-nine years and his grandfather before them.

From his tiny greenhouse he hatches 1000 plants a year, mostly bedding, in aid of community causes such as the Grasmere Best Kept Village Competition and the Conservative Club – for whom he recently sold sixty of his Busy Lizzies on a Saturday morning. He also gives a lot away to friends. Every year he promises himself that he must cut down on these bedding plants: 'They're such a lot of work, aren't they? As you get older, laziness gets the better of you.' So he picks up his seed catalogue and says 'I'll not have this and I'll not have that', but when he comes to add them up he has thirty-six packets of seed. He had them all in his hands, that winter afternoon, shuffling them together with his fingers, itching to get them sown. He couldn't take his eyes off the packet of petunias he was going to plant along the edge of the lawn instead of the alyssum he had there last summer. 'Very disappointing. The white ones were all right, but the coloured ones were dreadful!'

He has recently become Executor for a neighbouring farmer's Estate, and the first thing he did before selling the land was to slap a covenant on forty acres banning the planting of any conifers. Conifers are generally destested by Cumbrian local people because they deface the landscape. 'When you're inside a conifer forest and walking

LOOKING TOWARDS THE 'LION AND THE LAMB'

amongst them, they're so thickly planted you see nothing but sky. You don't see anything growing on the forest floor either because, unlike broadleaved woods, no light gets in so nothing grows.'

Apart from gardening John has always been interested in wild flowers. When, as Executor, he was allowed to choose a portion of the Estate to keep, he chose sixteen and a half acres of fellside above his house where he set about making a wild flower sanctuary bordering a stream.

He walks to the bottom of his garden every single morning to 'see how things are doing, how they're growing' and on to his greenhouse to water the seedlings. Seventy now, he'll carry on as long as he can and then, 'When I'm too old, then I'm too old. It's a lot of work, but it's very nice to walk around your garden; I don't care what anybody says. All that colour!'

What he doesn't like are unwelcome visitors. Woe befall any of Peter Rabbit's relations should they disobey mother and help themselves to this modern Mr McGregor's delectable array of flowers and vegetables. For John is up at 5 a.m. in the summertime and at his bedroom window with binoculars focused on the comings and goings all round the garden 'to see if there's anything in there that shouldn't be in' – like a pair of long, pointed ears sticking up amongst the plants. 'I had one bloomin' rabbit last summer who was digging holes all over the garden faster than I was filling them in. He ate a whole patch of young delphiniums clear off – the whole blinkin' lot and rock roses, too, doing more damage in one single night as it takes months to grow.'

The Mr McGregors of today are a sharper breed, for the old Mr McGregor never caught anything more than Peter's dimwitted father. But times have changed. While John slips quietly out the back door and climbs over the fence into the fellside field, 'Mrs McGregor' opens the front door. This startles the rabbits and they bolt out of the garden and up the fell towards the woods where a certain person is already waiting for them. And does 'Mrs McGregor' still make rabbit pie? Well, she used to make rabbit casserole but when mixamatosis came along, it put her off.

John and Betty's garden overlooks Helm Crag, the most famous fell in Lakeland and a good talking point for the tourists, for on its summit etched against the sky is the rocky silhouette of a lion lying down with a lamb between its paws. Not only is it an optical illusion, it's a romantic one as well. Many things have changed in the Lake District, but not all. The lion will never lie down with the lamb any more than Mr McGregor would befriend a rabbit.

Although John now lives in Grasmere, his heart will always belong to the Hawkshead of his youth. Every morning, until he drops, he'll walk to the bottom of his garden, stalking his terrain, a king among men.

M I R E S Y K E
L O W E S W A T E R

J o a n   L a s k e y

Iset off one cloudy day to find a particular garden in Loweswater I vaguely remembered mentioned in a horticultural journal and, although I peered into
every garden I could see in all of Loweswater, I could not find it.

Driving along by the lake, frustrated by this wasted journey, I suddenly
saw a dirt track leading up the fell through woods. A hunch, a sharp right and half a
mile later, there it was. Not the garden I had been looking for but the one I was meant to
find.

The farmhouse had a French look about it of faded chalky stone and overlooked
the garden which had grown outwards from the buttresses of old barns. Under a pearly-
grey sky the colours were so delicate that when I glanced past the garden across the lake
and beyond to a fell of bracken, grass and heather, it looked like a muted dream.

A jazzy black and white dalmatian bounded out of the house to greet me, and her
barking brought Joan Laskey to the gate. She didn't seem in the least surprised to see a
total stranger on her doorstep. I introduced myself and explained about my ideas for
this book as we stepped into the garden. 'I suppose a garden is a hole to bolt into,' she
said slowly, 'in it you try to create your ideal world – or what you imagine your ideal
world to be. But when you achieve it, it's claustrophobic.'

It did not surprise me to learn that Joan practises Client Centred Counselling – a
non-directive approach aimed at helping people to come to terms with their problems
through self-realization. Joan believes that in working with people, acceptance of the
individual without expectations is important.

'It's arbitrary why we're here – I don't see any plan. I don't think we're any more
important than the dogs, cats, plants, amoeba, whatever. I said that recently to a friend
who was feeling really washed up and she said, "You have no idea how wonderful that
makes me feel that I might not be any more important than anything else." What a load
we put on people's lives. Civilization, ideas of religion, no wonder we have nervous
breakdowns. I find it odd that one should find oneself so important.'

Is gardening therapeutic? Joan laughed. 'If you like gardening, it's therapeutic
and if you don't, it isn't! Anything that takes you out of yourself and stops you from
going around in circles inside is therapeutic. If I were to sit down and think about

myself I would go rapidly off the wall with boredom. I can't easily contain boredom. I'm better off with both my hands and my mind busy.'

The most striking thing about Joan's garden is how the plants are actively thriving and not merely surviving. It's not a wild garden but it seems so natural you're hardly aware a hand has guided secateurs, fork or spade. I asked her if she was satisfied with it. 'Oh no,' she said, 'once your garden is perfect, it's time to move. The worst thing is being satisfied. Once you're satisfied, you might as well be dead.' The garden looked perfect to me, the kind of garden a child would remember nostalgically later on.

'The garden at Miresyke is a small one of about a quarter of an acre and its character has been dictated by its position on a fellside above Loweswater Lake, overlooking the fells on the opposite side, and also by its construction in a garth backed by old stone farm buildings. It is therefore quite unmistakably a farmhouse garden and I have tried to marry these two aspects of the environment in the way the garden has taken shape and in the plants I grow.

'Gardening in Cumbria, particularly in the Lake District, is a matter of coming to terms with excesses: excessive wind, excessive rain and above all, excessive growth. Catalogues compiled in drier parts of the country give the uninitiated no hint of the ultimate state of lush growth that can be attained in the course of a season and to avoid a complete mess of wind-battered overgrowth in August, great care must be exercised in the choice of plants and shrubs.

'My love of gardening grew out of a keen interest, from an early age, in wild plants, so that my choice of plants for the garden comes down heavily on the side of those which grow wild in some part of the world and of old-fashioned garden plants and herbs which have a simplicity that suits both my taste and the surroundings.

'The climate here seems to suit Chinese and Himalayan plants very well. I am not a lover of rhododendrons and have only one, which was a present, but *Mahonia japonica* and *Rosa moyesii* dominate their particular patch and *Magnolia stellata* is another Asian which does very well. *Arisaema candidissima* increases fast on its natural slate and the blue poppies thrive, as do the Asiatic gentians. However, because the garden faces south with a gritty soil, I can grow some of the less demanding sun-lovers – pinks, some alpines, irises and old-fashioned shrub roses, although all these have to be carefully selected, through trial and error, for resistance to damp.

'As the rainfall is so high and in this garden, because of its microclimate the incidence of frost not great, I have found it necessary to use ground cover extensively to combat the perpetual growth of weeds. Violets, violas and the more colourful bugles are high among my favourites.

'Finally, because they do so well, I grow a range of small bulbs, species crocus,

THE STILL AND MUTED DREAM OF A FARMHOUSE
GARDEN OVERLOOKING LOWESWATER

dog's tooth violets, fritillarias and various forms of anemone, as well as the shorter-growing varieties of narcissus species. These are all tucked in between shrubs and herbaceous plants to extend the flowering time in the garden.

'Ideally, I think the garden should be a creative expression of the gardener's personality, combining a love of plants with a feeling for design and a sensitivity to the surroundings. The degree to which one succeeds in amalgamating these three elements determines the sense of harmony which the garden achieves. I am still working on it!'

FLYING BUTTRESSES LEND DRAMA AND TEXTURE

The Dream Fulfilled

Four Oaks
Warwick Bridge

Edith Dickman

'Gardens are for sharing,' everyone will tell you, but they don't expect you to open up your gates to provide food and shelter for the masses. Most of us create a garden with an eye on the welfare of wildlife and a nod to the special requirements within the family, but primarily to paint a satisfying picture for ourselves. Edith Dickman's garden, however, has been given over to some rather special citizens and, although they are quite numerous, fortunately they are also quite small and don't take up too much space.

Until ten years ago, Edith and John Dickman lived most of their married life near Bromley. It was their dream to return north to their roots – his on the Solway Firth, and hers by the Roman Wall – on their retirement. But their dream was blown away by John's sudden death. Edith suddenly found herself a widow, with two married daughters and a third about to leave home for university.

Bee keeping had been her husband's hobby. Edith had never done anything more than follow him round holding the smoker, and when he died she wanted to give them up. But the local bee keepers persuaded her to keep them and taught her how to care for them. By the end of the first year she had won two first prizes for her honey. 'Very important,' she said firmly, 'to have a hobby like that when you live alone.' She also had enough perspective on life to decide she would move back north and start afresh.

It certainly is bee heaven. They've got pride of place – the warmest, sunniest, most sheltered spot in the garden. When Edith first arrived, she waited for a while to see what would come up and when nothing did she felt free to plant her pollen and nectar garden. Providing ambrosia for bees would in turn produce fine-tasting honey for her.

Crocuses, snowdrops and daffodils greet the bees in spring, followed by an array of

delectables, such as lavender, rosemary and marjoram (said to improve the flavour of the honey), and many other herbs. Rock plants such as aubretia and arabis are great favourites because they produce an abundance of little flowers. Edith likes a scented garden, so old roses, philadelphus, *Viburnum fragrans*, buddleia, lavatera, malva and hypericum all have a place. There is a heather garden, a herb garden, a vegetable

AN ORNAMENTAL HIVE

patch and a fruiting patch of raspberries, gooseberries and blackcurrants on which the bees do a good job and she gets a bumper crop. Useful to both bee and bee mistress is the herb alecost, which supplies food for the bees and acts on a bee sting like a dock leaf on a nettle sting.

Life inside a beehive is not for the faint-hearted but it fascinates Edith. The individual is ruthlessly sacrificed for the common good and the survival of the colony is paramount. One interesting peculiarity bees have is that they don't mix their drinks, so to speak. Once they start on a particular plant they will stay on that blossom, flying past every other temptation.

Edith's bees are quite safe inside her garden – naturally she uses only safe pesticides or sprays – but keeping bees in the north of England is doubly difficult, not only because of the short growing season but because of new methods of farming. No meadow flowers are left because making hay when there's no sun to shine is impossible so farmers have opted to make silage instead. Clover used to be the main crop for honey but modern farming has banished it so there's very little English honey left at all. Oil seed rape is a good supply of food for bees but, although the farmers are supposed to ring the Bee Keepers' Association in the area and warn them when they're spraying pesticides and so on, they don't always do it and many bees die because they are not shut in. Farmers are not supposed to spray when the blossom is out, but they sometimes do. Edith was particularly irate about a marvellous crop of dandelions the bees were feeding on by the roadside which the farmer killed completely, and the bees with it. Farming practices are often so appalling from the bees' point of view that the best place to keep bees is thought to be on the edge of a city with trees, gardens and weeds!

Edith believes in educating people about how to grow plants safely. She lectures at Women's Institutes and always begins by saying 'Now you know all of the work of the world is done by women and so it is with the bees.' A local broadcaster once wandered

in as she was holding a meeting in the pub, and the next thing Edith knew she was broadcasting her message on national radio.

It is said that people don't change and this wasn't the first time she had made the best of a bad situation: 'My first attempt at gardening was when I was about seven and we lived on an old farm with flagstones around the front of the house. My job on a Saturday morning was to scrub those wretched flagstones and put white edge on them with chalk. Nobody ever went to the front door of the farm – they all had to go to the back. My Mother was very Victorian. We all had our jobs to do and this was mine. I really hated it because I had to use cold water and it was horrible. One day I decided there could be a lovely garden there instead. There was a man employed on the farm and I asked him to help me. We lifted six flagstones here and six flagstones there and I quickly went out and planted some wallflowers or something. When the family came to after the initial shock, they all said: "Oh, isn't it nice to have some flowers." It was only a couple of feet or so wide all the way along but I didn't have to scrub those horrid stones any more. So that was my first garden.'

This may be Edith's last garden, this bee heaven born of personal loss and courage which she has made the best of, in this the best of all possible worlds.

BEE HEAVEN IN THE HERB GARDEN

L E V E N S   H A L L
K E N D A L

H a l   a n d   S u s a n   B a g o t

I f ever there were a dream garden, this is it, for Levens is a magical garden of fantasy and imagination. It was cubist, surrealist and abstract 250 years before Picasso, Dali and Henry Moore reinvented them and I shouldn't be surprised if Lewis Carroll hadn't found his inspiration for *Alice in Wonderland* strolling amongst topiary with names such as the King and Queen of Chess, the Howard Lion, Judge's Wig and Portuguese Lantern. The great shapes have grown huge and eccentric; they are venerable old souls who are far more mystical to me than the monoliths of Stonehenge because they are alive and still growing.

It is hard to believe now that Levens was dreamt up by two enterprising young fellows when their boss resigned and they were made redundant. The year was 1689, the 'boss' was King James II and the two friends were Colonel James Grahme, adventurer and courtier who shared the King's mistress, and his great gardener, Monsieur Guillaume Beaumont. It is said that Colonel Grahme won Levens Hall from his cousin on a gambling table and after the King's abdication, the Colonel returned north to his roots, taking Monsieur Beaumont with him.

Colonel Grahme and Monsieur Beaumont laid out the intricate topiary in the parterre but also experimented with the innovative ideas of their friend, the diarist John Evelyn, who had theories about 'improving the landscape' by transforming it into parkland with open vistas and strategically positioned groves of trees.

Money was short, there wasn't always enough to pay the wages and so the creation of Levens was a labour of love. Beaumont is reported to have become extremely excited by finding the 'richest mould that ever we have seen'. In 1701, a freak October storm blew down over 700 trees in the parkland and garden, heralding a sad decade in which Mrs Grahme was to die, the house nearly burn down and which brought the death of the Colonel's second wife. A devastated Beaumont took to drink and although he continued to work in the garden he was never the same again. Witnessing these tragedies was the Colonel's elder daughter, Catherine, who later became the Countess of Suffolk and Berkshire. After the Colonel's death, Catherine's husband inherited Levens but as he had many other estates to look after he did not seek change.

Topiary and formal garden design in general had by then become most un-

DELPHINIUMS BY THE ELIZABETHAN MANSION

fashionable but Catherine did not make any attempt to dig up the parterre. The happy memories of her childhood lay in that garden and Catherine refused to change it.

The next occupier of Levens was Catherine's daughter-in-law, the widowed Viscountess Andover. For forty-seven years, she and her gardener, Macmillan, let the garden grow wild. The topiary was around 100 years old by then and, under the Viscountess's benign neglect, became a secret garden of wild roses, mignonette and honeysuckle; the topiary and box were set free to enjoy a riotous adolescence in Mr Beaumont's exceedingly good mould. What a task greeted the next heiress, who had nine miles of box to replant. Luckily for Levens, she had married a Bagot.

The Bagot coat of arms has a goat emblazoned on it, a symbol of tenacity and practical idealism. Legend has it that after the Bagots fought long and hard for King Richard during the Crusades they were rewarded with lands – and also with a witty novelty present of a few Swiss goats. Although Hal Bagot, the present owner of Levens, will tell you that they have a 'great propensity for dying', their original goats' progeny are still around, 500 years later, a group of thirty 'wild, woolly and beautiful creatures' moving decoratively through the park.

Hal and Susan Bagot, like all the Bagots before them, feel they have to keep the goats going, with the same compulsion that they keep Levens as a family home. Each

A SURREALIST GARDEN OF SOFT SCULPTURE

generation falls under its spell even though the inheritance is not the gift it once was. Yet topiary is once again popular and Levens is often now featured in books, magazines and television commercials. The garden has rallied through two great social curses: fashion and modern planning.

Levens' future seems secure. An organ plays cheerfully in the car park alongside the traditional attractions of brightly polished steam and traction engines. The magnificent Elizabethan mansion and gardens are beautifully presented to a grateful public – over 37,000 visit every year. Snooping through the Visitors' Book, I found little treasures. A fellow from Carlisle wrote, 'It has taken me thirty-five years to get here – why did I wait so long?' and, from Brixton, 'If you sellin' we buyin'!'. 'Wonderful topophilia,' wrote a man from Morecambe, and Steve Cram, the British runner, noted, 'Only took me a minute to get round!' From America, 'The most beautiful bushes I've ever seen,' and lastly, 'Head gardener needs a haircut.'

The head gardener's name is Chris Crowder and he's only twenty-six. He trained at the Royal Botanic Gardens, Kew, and wanted to work in a garden with a sense of history. A keen climber and potholer, Chris is ideally suited to abseiling from the 100-foot tower to deal with overgrown ivy or to hang off scaffolding and clip the enormous beech and yew hedges. And, like most of the other people who've been involved with

SHAPE AND TEXTURE AGAINST A WALL OF GREEN

Levens, Chris has an original mind. 'If you're into my personal philosophy about gardens,' he tells me, 'I'm sort of in two minds about whether it's cruel to do any gardening at all.' This may sound peculiar but it only means that to him a weed is as beautiful as any other plant. This is just the sort of person Levens needs, for the best gardeners are those who respect nature in all its forms. He has his own vision with which to carry the gardens into the twenty-first century, for although topiary lives a long time it is not immortal. Young plants are being planted in some of the gaps left by early demises and they will be left to grow freely for five years before being clipped into shapes. 'This way, people will be able to see how it's done – it's something you can have a go at yourself.'

Chris would like to make Levens known for more than just topiary – he wants to make it a plantsman's garden, full of rare and interesting trees and plants. He spends many weekends visiting gardens around the country, collecting seeds and cuttings which he has bubbling away in his nursery beds. This side of the garden is developing fast and quietly gaining ground alongside its famous neighbour, the topiary.

'The loveliest thing about it,' says Susan Bagot, Hal's vivacious wife, is 'emptying children in there. They always see something new in the shapes and rush and say, "I've just seen the Mad Hatter's top hat or something".' Levens Hall is really a child's garden and it appeals to all of us who are children at heart.

D A L E M A I N
U L L S W A T E R

S y l v i a   M a r y   M c C o s h

Dalemain has belonged to the family of Sylvia Mary Hasell McCosh since 1679 and she is as much a part of it as the pele tower or the spring aconites. To the manor she may have been born but she and her husband, Bryce, have worked harder to keep it than the heirs who farmed and forested the 30,000-acre estate before her.

The house is impressive but not intimidating. Around the back, where house, grounds, stables and garden meet in the cobblestoned courtyard, there is an atmosphere of the village green. There you will find Mrs McCosh on Sunday mornings conducting the plant sales – labelling plants, chatting to people and offering advice. While you are making your choice in the courtyard, you will notice a large specimen of the old rose *Gloire de Dijon* flowering against the sandstone stable wall, the colour blending as subtly as Italian marble. It was planted there by 'Miss Sylvia' when she was seven. She rescued it from the ash pit where it had been cast out as was customary in those days for anything that wasn't growing well. Nourished by manure from the ponies and nurtured by Miss Sylvia, the rose has long outlasted the old gardener who threw it away and it is easily the most beautiful ornament in the courtyard. Dalemain is very much Mrs McCosh's garden and it is a garden of delights for much of the year. In spring there are carpets of aconites, snowdrops and crocuses; tulips in the Knot Garden; daffodils in the orchard. All sorts of shrubs and trees blossom in rapid succession as April drifts into May, bringing early roses and the magnificent blue Himalayan poppy, *Meconopsis grandis G.S. 600.*

May is a busy time for garden visiting in the Lake District. We reel around the rhododendron exotica of the other gardens to return to Dalemain where the classics of the English garden – old roses, delphiniums, catmint and peonies – steadily unfold in its 'clarty', alka-

A SHADY ALCOVE OF
WEATHERED STONE
AND FRESH FOLIAGE

CLASSIC ENGLISH PLANTS FRAME ULLSWATER FELLS

line soil. The herbaceous border along the terrace is wonderful as *Crambe cordifolia* reaches up to touch the climbing roses. Planted on the edge of the terrace, rambling roses grow in great profusion, spreading out towards the rolling hills and clouds.

Mrs McCosh comes from a long line of gardeners. Her great-grandmother and great aunts were passionate gardeners. Her mother also gardened, though in fits and starts, but her particular contribution was christening the wood at the end of the top garden 'Lob's Wood'. Lob was a puckish character from J. M. Barrie's play *Dear Brutus*, who had a wonderful garden. Every Midsummer's Eve, Lob invited a group of unhappy 'if only' guests who regretted 'the spoken word, the past life, and the neglected opportunity'. They were sent into the magic wood beyond the garden and given another chance to live their lives but they all relived their mistakes. Mrs Hasell en-

couraged her daughters to garden by the door into Lob's Wood, perhaps to impress upon them that their destiny lay not in the hands of fate but in their own.

Mrs McCosh has gardened ever since she was a little girl. She and her sister filled their little gardens by Lob's Wood with rescued plants and seeds. While Nanny sat in the shade of the open summer house knitting, they tended their sunbeaten patches, 'carrying horrid little watering cans of water up from a tap half-way down the path' until it was time for lunch. This did nothing to diminish the enthusiasm of a little girl whose first love was wild flowers. Growing up in a place that was quite isolated and where people still went shopping in a dog cart and pony trap, all Mrs McCosh's diversions lay outside her front door. There were tea parties in the stables and botanical expeditions with her governess, Miss Murray, across fields and up fells looking for wild flowers such as the rare white violet. Noting them and pressing them in her nature books became part of the 'schoolroom curriculum'.

The first gardener at Dalemain that she remembers was Will Stuart, who arrived in 1891 and died there when she was twenty-two. She would watch him prune the roses on the terrace. 'What are you doing, Stuart?' she is reputed to have asked him at the age of six.

'Pruning, Miss Sylvia.'

'When will the prunes be ripe?' she replied.

CRAMBE CORDIFOLIA – AN EMBROIDERY OF WHITE LACE

Paeony lobata 'Sunshine' in the kitchen garden

She left Dalemain to be married and moved to Huntfield in Biggar, Scotland. When Mrs McCosh's father died in 1972, Dalemain became hers, the first heiress. Her loyalties were not so much divided as doubled. She and her husband kept their Huntfield home whilst restoring Dalemain which eventually necessitated opening it to the public. Her husband took over the management of the estate and she threw herself into saving the garden which had 'got into a frightful mess under several indifferent gardeners'. The Top Garden, where she'd had her childhood patch, was 'just dirty old vegetables and thriving asparagus', which her father had loved. It is now filled with old roses – damask, gallica, species, briars – Dalemain is well known for its collection. The boxwood Knot Garden which dates from Tudor days was originally a herb garden and they have turned it into a scented garden.

Sixteen years later, Mrs McCosh still divides her time between her two homes which she has charmingly written about in her book *Between Two Gardens*. Opening your garden to the public is a big responsibility at the best of times, but especially difficult as she is just recovering from meningitis which she contracted three years ago. But there's nothing like a grateful and admiring public to give one the incentive to keep it all going. And then there are little incidents which amuse her like being taken for the gardener and being told 'I hope you're well paid'.

'It is a divine garden,' comments one of Lob's houseguests in the play. 'How lovely it is in the moonlight. Roses, roses, all the way. It is like a hat I had once when I was young. Lob is such an amazing gardener, I believe he could even grow hats.'

H O W   G H Y L L
A P P L E T H W A I T E

M i s s   V e r a   D i x o n

Vera Dixon is well over eighty. We don't know exactly how much and we don't like to ask. She grew up in Leicester where she and her sister lived at home until she retired from nursery school teaching sixteen years ago and moved to Keswick. Since then she has worked devotedly at the Oxfam shop where I first got to know her. On Saturday mornings she would leave freshly dug clumps of cottage garden plants outside the shop for the princely sum of fifteen pence. This is like leaving cheese out for the mice at night. By half-past nine the clumps had vanished and the keen gardeners of Keswick were staggering around town laden not only with plants but with other bits and pieces from the Oxfam shop which had caught their eye.

'There's something in common with all people who love their plants, I think. You can talk to them and you can give them bits of cuttings and things to make a sort of atmosphere. It's like giving away bits of yourself. And I suppose those people are like that because their parents – like my mother and father – cared for plants.

'When I was quite small we had a very dear friend who was a gardener. He had a wife. She died. I didn't see her. But he had a son too, and the son was killed in the First World War. My mother was very kind to him. She used to invite him every Saturday to come to our house and he played chess or whist with my father.

'I think that was the start of it. He worked for a lady who had a big garden and I used to follow him around the glasshouses looking at the different plants and he'd

VERA DIXON IN LATE SUMMER

tell me what they were and what he gave them to make them grow. He became quite well-known in Leicester for the plants he grew in these glasshouses. There were three in a row. One was quite cool, the next was a bit warmer and the last one you came to was really quite hot which I thought was rather exciting. That was the

beginning of the garden episode.

'At school we used to do a lot of growing from seeds, and my mother, particularly, was very interested in flowers and plants. We had a vegetable plot. People grew a lot of vegetables then because things were a bit difficult after the First World War. My mother wasn't interested just in the plants but in all of nature – like respect for other people's feelings. I know some people who used to think that this splendid gardener we knew was "only a gardener". But he was a great reader and he loved his plants. His philosophy was never to pass up nature. He preserved it as much as he could because of his care of plants.

'I remember seeing him standing at the top of a ladder over a big arch of rhododendrons and he'd be on the top of these things, pruning them, and I was thinking how clever he was. He had a great effect on me by the way he cared for things, not just because they were rather special but because they were plants which I've always felt deserved being cared for because they were God's living creatures. He didn't exactly say that but it was his attitude towards his plants.

'I tried to instil this in my pupils when I was a teacher – directing them towards an attitude to something, not telling them what they should think about it. They should see that the plants themselves have special virtues or a special place in their lives. If they're of a certain nature they grow into a daffodil or whatever just like we grow into

the person we were supposed to be. Smallish children soon understand. You say, come and look at this, and they really are interested. They get to like them even if they hadn't before because they're growing under their feet really.

'I came to the Lake District with my sister when we retired. We always used to come up here for walking. We saw the house which we have now. It had rather a nice atmosphere as though people lived in it and loved it so: although it's shabby, it's loving. The garden had been quite well looked after. We didn't put all the plants in – just some of them. The lady who lived here before, her husband was a retired doctor and she was very fond of the garden. She loved the stream and she put plants in that like the stream too. It's lovely. It goes "whoosh" when we've had a lot of rain and once or twice it's gone right over the bridge. I often think of her and say "You would have liked this garden" because she really cared, like real flower owners do.

'I just like the garden as a garden. The plants are individuals. I'm quite apart from it. I just stand there and look at it. I think small plants are perhaps more endearing than rather big plants. I'm not so fond of big flowers that say "Look at me!" and, of course, the colours are sometimes more desirable in smaller plants.

'I like the little wee ones, the early spring ones like a little snowdrop coming up, turning its head down. Or the ones that come as surprises – ones you didn't expect to see. They always seem to know where to put themselves.

'I used to have a lot of catalogues come to the house – don't know how they got here. But you can't say "I'll have this and I'll have that because perhaps they won't like the place you put them in unless you're very careful. I don't choose things. They choose to come into my garden. There's thousands of seeds floating about our garden now because I'm cutting a lot of dead stalks down and out come all the seeds. I try to let them please themselves where they go. I just let them have their own way. Not all. I don't allow all, and I weed a bit. Some plants look a bit miserable when you try to make them grow in a certain place. Those that grow on their own look happier. I put them in a place I think they'll like with sunshine or shade or whatever. And then if they don't grow in one season, I say – "Oh, you don't like my garden," or, "You're having a rest this year. You don't want to grow any flowers, you just want to be left. Feel a bit better next year."

'I try to be philosophical and say "Well, all right," and give up and try something else. And we have to do it ourselves, more or less, in life – accept what comes, even if it doesn't seem to be the best thing for us.'

Vera has had to give up her work at the Oxfam shop as well as opening her garden every spring for a children's charity. But despite her increasingly frail health and the loss of her sister, she continues to love her garden.

E D E N   V A L L E Y

Victor   and   Sarah - Anne ' s   Garden

I was pottering along one afternoon going nowhere in particular when I came to a little house in the village of Great Salkeld near Penrith. It had a marvellous display of sweet peas along the front fence obscuring the house and the whole family was working in the garden. I took a few pictures and explained what I was doing. When I had finished, George Martindale, the owner, said quietly, 'I don't like flowers much, are you interested in vegetable gardens? I know one down the road.'

I followed his Reliant Robin car down a discreetly hidden winding lane deep into the beautiful Eden Valley past the charming manor house with a front garden wrapped up in yew hedges, delphiniums, verbascum and foxgloves poking over the tops in gay profusion.

We parked behind the farm buildings. George's large vegetable garden melted into the landscape of green and gold. He had managed this 300-acre farm for thirty years and when he retired he was given this patch to tend. It was immaculate and gleamed in the sun, his compost heap a work of art. I left with an armful of broad beans, most of which I ate on the way home.

It wasn't long before I was there again, this time to see Sarah-Anne who to the manor married. She is everything you expect when you imagine the quintessential Englishwoman: attractive, informed, discreet, humorous. She left me alone to photograph. I felt what must have been the atmosphere of Sissinghurst and Hidcote before their creators left and the public moved in. This other Eden embodied the rare art of looking completely natural yet full of interestingly shaped plants and harmonious colours. It was a visual surprise. It was magic. This was rural life at its best, far from cold comfort farm, far from the madding crowds of big cities. Again, I arrived home empty-handed, having scoffed Sarah-Anne's present of spinach and rocket, my favourite salad herb. You can imagine my surprise when, on unfolding our local paper a few months later, I saw Sarah-Anne on the front page welcoming the Princess of Wales here as the wife of the High Sheriff of Cumbria!

'My first recollections were not so much of gardening as a passion for wild flowers. I used to be taken for walks by my Nanny. She would push my brother in the pram and I would identify any flower I didn't know with a wild flower book given to me by my father. This was in Sussex where we lived for the first six years of my life. Then, partly

because of the war and partly because of the fact that my father had inherited a house in the north of England – near Newby Bridge – my mother, three children and young Nanny moved here for safety. My mother was Austrian and it was difficult for her, being a young foreign girl in a large, dilapidated but lovely Georgian house, in an area where she didn't know anybody. My father was killed in the war and she knuckled down and started farming, knowing nothing about it and not speaking the language very well, let alone understanding the Cumbrian dialect. There was not much of a conventional garden at this house but there was a large, walled kitchen garden of an acre, which my mother ran as a market garden without much success.

'Victor and I married in 1960. We lived in a small rented house near Little Salkeld and we struggled with rather an unruly garden choked with ground elder and twitch [couch grass]. All our children were born there and, after seven years, we bought a house in Great Salkeld – the other side of the river, and much more convenient for the farm where Victor has always farmed. It had a lovely walled garden at the back and this was the first time we had somewhere where we could create something of our own, and it was then that it all became such fun.

'We made a big lawn for the children to play on. My husband planted a curved beech hedge with two archways at one end of the lawn and there were shrubs and shrub roses at the other end. We planted roses and clematis to grow up the walls and through the trees and made two herbaceous borders in the walled garden on one side and grew vegetables on the other side. Victor particularly likes growing things in rows, and had a very good grounding from his mother on digging and mucking [manuring] the ground.

'My taste at this time was for ordinary cottage garden plants – bright colours and easy to grow – and I greedily wanted flowers that would smell nice and would pick well. I am now seeing how rewarding it is to grow things such as day lilies that do neither of these things but which flower for ages, and I have also grown to love the more unusual plants that already grow here and different species of the things I already knew.

'After fifteen years at Great Salkeld we moved to my husband's parents' house, which had a ready-made, very much loved and cared for, mature garden. It was getting slightly out of hand so we had to try to make it more manageable, as we have no help except occasionally with mowing. The garden has been beautifully thought out as there is always colour to enjoy throughout the year. We can't create a new garden here so much – it's more a question of cutting the work back but it is beginning to feel like our garden now. Even though I'm sure my mother-in-law cannot approve of everything we do, she is none the less very nice about it. I think she found leaving the garden harder than leaving the house; she had been here for fifty years.

'So far, the biggest change has been Victor's taming of the walled garden. He has

George Martindale and his work of art
(Previous page) Poppies, verbascum and potentilla

planted flowers along and up the walls and has made a pattern of grass with a hexago-
nal paved area in the middle; perhaps this will have a bower covered in roses one day.
He can still have his lines of vegetables and I'm hoping next year he'll grow some ornamental kale as well as red lettuce and purple beans.

'My husband takes care of the vegetable garden – and I the flowers. Lopping off
branches is done together amidst much heated argument, as I love trailing branches
and spreading plants and he likes them regimented and trimmed to make mowing
easier! We both adore the garden and, with a few exceptions, gardening. There is
nothing more therapeutic than an hour or two's weeding. To go to the top of the garden
on a warm evening and stand under the spreading, hanging branches of the cut-leaf
lime when in flower is like being in a beehive surrounded by the smell of honey and the
buzzing of bees.

'We have planted a number of specimen trees as there is always a disaster over the
winter. I think the big cobbled yard at the back has become more colourful since we've
been here, with roses climbing the north-facing wall of the house and lots of troughs and
pots containing lilies. The kitchen opens its french windows on to a square, enclosed

garden divided into four by flagged paths and surrounded by yew hedges.

'As for what the garden means to me now the children have gone away – it seems to dominate our lives, although we swore we wouldn't let it. About twice a year I feel as if the garden is taking me over and I can't keep up with it but we wouldn't be without it. It is a never-ending pleasure to go round it with long-suffering friends and explain every plant. What would there be to live for if it wasn't for the garden springing into life each year? Even in February, I can plant the sweet peas and feel that I am doing something.

'I certainly feel that gardens are reasons for going to houses and even more for leaving them. We will probably have to leave this one when the work gets too much. The hardest thing is to leave a garden knowing that the next people won't love it as you do. At least my mother-in-law must know that although we may not be as knowledgeable as she is, we are enthusiastic and love it.'

T H E   O L D   M I L L
T H U R S T O N F I E L D

J e a n   T h o m a s

It was a patch of vibrant 'Evelyn Fison' roses flowering against the whitewashed wall of an old millhouse that stopped my car here on a hazy October afternoon. The sound of a clicking camera brought Jean Thomas to the gate and after a brief exchange she invited me into her garden. She was in the middle of her autumn clearing and I just caught the garden before it vanished. October gardens have a lovely muted feel to them, the colours deepening before fading away.

Life has not always been easy for Jean; in fact nothing has ever been freely given to her. She's learned to be philosophical about life and has developed a very positive and open attitude, believing that a closed mind is the worst thing to have and that life is a constant struggle towards tolerance and patience.

She was brought up in the beautiful market town of St Albans in Hertfordshire. The house was set in an old orchard and she grew up playing in the trees, admiring blossom and gathering fruit. She joined de Havillands as a secretary where she met her husband Tom, a rocket engineer who was then working on a guided missile project. His later work on Blue Streak took them and their sons to Australia and then to the north of England. Defence cutbacks in 1973 made Tom redundant and the demand for rocket engineers was non-existent, so for a couple of years they were thrown back on their own resources. 'There were times,' Jean says, 'when if we didn't grow it, we didn't eat it. We had to be completely self-sufficient and this was a great learning curve as to what we could and couldn't do. We got by and learned how to barter. If we wanted anything we could barter our oven-ready poultry. Our local radio had something called Swap Shop. No money was involved. I was after some flagstones once when we were busy trying to put a path down in the garden and in exchange for a few flagstones they would have whatever we had that was surplus.

'We had eleven lorry-loads of "spoil" to build up the big flower beds. It took years of making compost and digging it in and getting farmyard manure to vitalize the soil. We grow many traditional cottage garden flowers as well as roses, dahlias and lilies to provide contrast, textures and scents. Borage, comfrey and nasturtiums proliferate each year and keep the bees and insects happy. We also set up a large vegetable garden

because it was important that we looked after ourselves and we'd always brought up the boys to believe that the man who can survive in a catastrophe is the man who can live off the land. I think one year we grew twenty-eight different types of vegetables.

'Tom had to go on the dole for a while because we had no money left at all. One can't be totally self-sufficient because one has to pay rates, electricity and water rates. I can't go into the civic centre and say, "Here's three tons of potatoes, will you let me off the rates?" So one has to have some earning capacity but there is a lot one can do without. We shopped in Oxfam before Oxfam was fashionable and the boys became very self-sufficient. Between them both there's very little they can't do.

'Tom likes growing vegetables. He's not terribly interested in fiddling on with the flowers but likes to see the end result in summer when the whole garden is a mass of colour. He puts the vegetables in and he harvests. He grows tomatoes – I don't do anything in the greenhouse, that's his domain, but I do the rest of the gardening. I like the peace. I like the fact that one can go out there and be at peace. One can sit and see so much going on. Even on a cold winter's day there's always something new to be seen.

DEEPENING AUTUMN COLOUR

GLORIOUS DISPLAY OF DAHLIAS IN SEPTEMBER SUN

'We have tried to make our rambling garden into one which satisfies many interests while keeping the balance between conservation of the wild area, self-sufficiency and the delight of flowers and bulbs. We have the flowers that give pleasure to anyone who likes gardening, and then there's the sharing of plants. A bonus of the garden is the friendship that it represents. But the garden is not just for us. It is arrogant to think that we are the sole inheritors of the earth and we forget that we depend so much on nature for keeping the balance. So we try to make sure that we maintain the ecology of the right trees, bushes and flowers, the wild flowers and the bog areas.

'We have spotted flycatchers who come each year from as far away as India and North Africa to nest in the *Parthenocissus* covering an old barn wall. Butterflies are a great favourite and the buddleias provide nectar for the Tortoiseshells, Red Admirals and Peacocks; Orangetips seem to prefer the lavender spikes. We feel we are blessed indeed to have a nice old cottage with a lovely ambience and space all round us. I can't think what sort of people we would be if we sat on top of a twenty-storey tower block with nowhere to garden at all.

'I think a garden reflects life. It has its hopes and its disappointments, rewards and joys. At the end of the season there's a quiet time and then there follows a time of regeneration and I think there's a simile there to life itself. One can learn so much if one has the time to stop, switch off, look and listen.'

73

H O L K E R H A L L
C A R K - I N - C A R T M E L

M r   a n d   M r s   H u g h
C a v e n d i s h

This is a garden of fulfilled visions. The product of two gardening enthusiasts having the resources, imagination, energy and taste to take a good garden and make it into a great one.

I am constantly rueing the past as I come across marvellous descriptions of gardens in their heyday for which I'm usually 100 years or so too late. The description of Muncaster Castle filled with thousands of Edwardian roses and all the glories of the South of France in her glasshouses made me ache when I read it. And what would anyone give for a time capsule to take us into the gardens of Vita Sackville-West or Lawrence Johnston when they, and not the general public, lived there.

Holker Hall is one of the few exceptions. It is a garden passing through its golden age: having inherited a sound past, it is now improving and expanding. It is a joy to photograph – vibrant, elegant, immaculate and exuberant. The cascade which was only a dream eighteen years ago was completed this year – and works! The Italianate formal garden which was designed to prolong the interest from woodland spring to herbaceous summer is now in its third year and reaching perfection.

The davidia planted seventeen years ago bloomed this spring for the first time and was smothered in bracts. And then there are the treats of the future to look forward to, such as the restoration of the Mawson-designed rose garden which is about to be planted up, and a bank of cornus including 'Eddie's White Wonder', eucryphias, a grove of myrtles and oxydendron, all planted and growing. Anticipating one's dotage, there are the magnolias to look forward to, planted but yet to reach their prime.

Holker has been blessed by good peaty soil and a wonderful micro-climate of mildness and moisture from the Gulf Stream so that even the tenderest shrubs survive. The other very important element is that it has never suffered periods of neglect. When you first drive in, the rolling Capability Brown-style parkland takes your breath away, but everything at Holker is on a grand scale. Most of the trees which can be seen today were

PEONIES IN THE SUMMER GARDEN

STONE URNS IN THE SUMMER GARDEN

planted by Lord George Cavendish who inherited the house in the mid-nineteenth century from his first cousin, a Lowther.

Lord George was a great gardener and grew seeds from a Cedar of Lebanon that was sent to him from the Holy Land, five of which grew into trees, and one of which still survives. He removed the topiary and informalized the planting so that, despite the grandeur of the house, the garden is a personal one. The architect of the woodland garden was Hugh's grandmother Lady Moyra, daughter of the tenth Duke of St Albans, and it fell to her daughter-in-law to preserve the garden during the terrible post-war years of death duties and taxation by providing a springboard for the next generation.

Hugh and Grania Cavendish are a glamorous couple and the Cumbrian equivalent of Harold and Vita. Sliding down the family tree, Hugh is cousin to the eleventh Duke of Devonshire so we know his roots are firmly in Holker soil. Grania is the stepdaughter of a botanist who brought her up while collecting plants all over the world, and the daughter of an artist who gardens with great abandon and vigour. Although she was born in the Bahamas and has lived in Africa, Italy, America and Suffolk, she has formed a real affection for the north of England. 'I love the north of England with a passion. I don't miss London. If I go south I can't wait to get back. The light here is wonderful. You get these long, long evenings and I love the climate. I love the access to the mountains and sea. I'd feel hemmed in anywhere else.'

Grania has been married eighteen years, has three children between seventeen and seven and she still looks about twenty. With the help of a very efficient administra-

tor, she runs the entire Holker enterprise which has a motor museum and a variety of attractions in keeping with a big Victorian house, and stages special events such as hot air ballooning, model aircraft and carriage driving trials. You'll find an adventure playground and a baby zoo here but no fruit machines. For his part, Hugh is deeply involved with the county council, hospice work and six different schools, and also runs a slate quarry business and various other companies to help finance Holker.

Their dream is to make Holker famous for its gardens. It's really rather exciting for us to have a little Sissinghurst brewing in England's back garden. 'There's a very unusual element here of partnership,' says Hugh; 'in most families one is much more interested than the other but we're both interested. Inevitably, there's a certain amount of conflict but it works and I think that what you get is rather like government and opposition.' The family motto *Cavendo Tutus* means look before you leap and, true to his blue blood, Hugh will tell you that 'gardening in a hurry is fatal. We do sort of discuss and look, discuss and look!'

'That's what's good about a garden this size,' says Grania. 'You can have a lot of plans evolving so you can put one into action while you're still thinking of others.'

Hugh remembers the garden as a small child and thinks a garden should be romantic, mysterious and enticing. And, being born here, he challenges any change. So when Arabella Lennox Boyd who advises them on the garden suggested they should remove a huge bank of rhododendron that was about to creep into the living room, Hugh nearly died of shock. But with hindsight they agree it was the best thing they did. 'A

VIEW FROM THE FORMAL GARDEN TO MORECAMBE BAY

whole group of trees can be growing and eventually obscure the whole view and you don't even notice it if you're living here,' they say.

Hugh is a purist with a slight preference for trees and shrubs. 'I love a garden in winter. There's an absolutely magic moment here I think, in February, when the garden is very, very tidy and stark, just before that sign of life. I've a passion for shape. It's an absolute mystery to me why some really beautiful plants which are not difficult to propagate have gone out of fashion like the New Zealand willow herb and *Buddleia alternifolia* 'Argentea'. They have acquired cuttings from the head gardener at the Chelsea Physic Garden, Jamie Compton, who has fired up their enthusiasm for South American plants.

Grania is a gardener after my own heart. 'I like not being able to see a square inch of earth. I like everything planted out and tumbling and full of scent'; flourishing in a happy marriage of Italian formalism and cottage garden opulence. Her vision will be realized in the rose garden which she wants to make romantic with arbours of shrub roses underplanted with lilies, *nepeta*, pinks, lavenders, prostrate and upright rosemaries, and clipped yew to give it substance. It will be surrounded by ornamental trees and eventually that too will be enlarged with another huge bed running all the way round it.

Grania believes it's important to grow things that thrive in a particular garden but 'sometimes plants that survive and flourish in one part of the garden might look unhappy in another and I believe in moving plants. If a plant is not doing well, move it. If it's moved at the right time with enough care and preparation, it's fine. It's also a question of caring for plants and loving them. We've been known to stand over a plant and say "Oh, this was a mistake" and three days later it's virtually given up.'

Her involvement with her garden is total. She doesn't feel she knows a plant until she's handled it and is amazed by people who live in London with no more garden than a window box and yet design gardens all over the world.

A LUTYENS BENCH AMONG *MECONOPSIS*

She often gets taken for the gardener, bottom up in a flower bed. 'I'll tramp through the new wing in my dungarees to get something and the guide will say "Good morning, Mrs Cavendish" and they'll all turn round and look past me because you're expected to be in a tea gown with lily-white hands, looking relaxed.'

78

H I G H   R I G G
G R A N G E - I N -
B O R R O W D A L E

M o l l y   B i r k e t t

Molly Birkett grew up just down the road from where she lives now in Portinscale. She read history at Cambridge and eventually became an Assistant Librarian at the London School of Economics. After nearly twenty years there, she found 'post-war London totally disagreeable', gave up a good job and returned to the Borrowdale valley bringing her friend Dorothea with her. Together they ran a guest house, spending several years compiling subject indexes of all the research being done in British Universities each year in history and social sciences. They had four months each year in which to catalogue thousands of entries, furiously working away all the winter.

Dorothea grew up in a musical family. When pressed, she revealed that Gustav Holst was her music teacher at St Paul's and persuaded her to take up the flute. When he wrote his Fugal Concerto for Oboe and Flute she was the first to play it! After Cambridge, she taught classics, did social work, went on to become the second secretary of the National Old People's Welfare Committee, now Age Concern, and bullied the local authorities on behalf of old people. She likes gardens but is not a 'natural gardener'. In their first house the garden was small and quite manageable but when they retired and moved to their present home the real work began. Dorothea was prevailed upon to help with the creation of this garden and she gamely weeded and killed bracken. But Molly is the real gardener.

They share a passion for music, particularly choral pieces, and as Hon Secretaries have been actively involved in the Cumbria Rural Choir, Dorothea for twenty years, Molly for four. Dorothea conducted Handel's *Messiah* with the Keswick Choral Society and a small orchestra until the onset of her blindness several years ago. Molly sings. Anything from Verdi's *Requiem* to Vaughan Williams, but the sounds don't come out quite like they used to. 'I don't know how much longer they're going to tolerate me,' she says with characteristic dry humour. Only one dream, to see the Taj Mahal, remains unfulfilled: 'I want to see it before I die.'

I first met Molly when she and Dorothea opened their garden for charity, in aid of

the Cumbria Rural Choir.

'If you inherit a love of gardening from your great-great-grandfather, famous for his gardening, and from your mother, whom you helped as long as you can remember, then you are ordained to be its slave all your life. All ardent gardeners are slightly mad, especially those who live in the Lake District. Here the scenery is so beautiful that it wrings your heart but the gardener must needs alter his little plot. Like an artist he has visions of colour and shape and, added to that, there is his love of individual plants. To achieve these visions he will toil endlessly against the odds, sometimes successfully but always driven on by other visions, other ideas. The world is his oyster for his plants come from far and wide and man-made hybrids are always tempting him to make plans and alterations. Wherever he goes he can enjoy and be tempted by other people's ideas, for no two people will develop the same type of area in the same way.

'In 1963, my friend and I were lucky enough to buy High Rigg, an acre on a hillside in the wettest part of the Lake District. Behind us oak wood, at the side gorse-strewn pasture. The bones of the garden were there, that is, the steep slope of the fellside, the hedges, a terrace, a fine holly, an over-run herbaceous border and a sensitive small planting of an apricot pink azalea, a *cypressus* and brilliant blue *lithospermum*. Elsewhere, brooms grew thickly and a Scots pine dominated the foreground. Blackberry, bracken and ground elder had taken advantage of the previous occupant who, at ninety-two, could no longer battle against them.

'Worst of all was the handsome but dread *polygonum cuspidatum*, against which she had waged war ceaselessly, even covering it with asphalt. Even less welcome, but firmly established, were plantings of *Rhododendron ponticum* which provided windbreaks but which could have been eliminated only by major excavations. Gradually, I realized what a constant source of irritation they could be. Always expanding by at least ten or fifteen inches a year, they have to be cut and cut again to keep them within bounds. The flower is thereby lost and their sensitive leaves make one feel colder than ever on a frosty night as they hang down, to hug themselves against the cold.

'As soon as we saw the house and garden, visions of a flowery meadow, a mini-wood, an herbaceous border, old-fashioned roses and a rock garden came in endless processions through my mind. It was obvious, too, that where there was a fall in the land to a natural basin there should be a pond, and leading to it a bog filled with salmon pink Bartley candelabra primulas and *Azalea kaempferi* (seen at the Saville gardens and always longed for).

'In 1963 there was an almost mythically good summer so we toiled endlessly against weeds. We sprayed bracken with a new wonder product (later withdrawn as being only partially successful), and dug and hacked the woody roots of the polygonum

and even seared the soil, two inches down to catch its smallest side roots. Later we were rewarded by the growth of the shrubs which enjoyed such soil treatment. Where we were to have a vegetable patch we found the soil was only a foot deep and the area was full of boulders as well as ash and other saplings.

'We found "the strong man of Keswick" and persuaded him to remove these and, as a bonus, to bring us several tons of topsoil from a newly built car park. This, after blocking a patch for several months, provided some root room for a few basic vegetables but they never enjoyed it and, when old age forced changes, shrubs replaced them.

'The top consideration in planning the garden was to make it harmonize with the hillside. Nothing could be too formal, and bright artificial colours such as Paul Scarlet geranium-red had to be avoided. It was also to be a bird and wild flower sanctuary.

'I read catalogues and gardening books endlessly and my talk became so intolerable that my friend took refuge in sleep when I began yet once again on the merits of Rhus 'Royal Purple' beside *Rosa cantabrigiensis* – or should it be a *Salix lanata* or would *Rhododendron* 'Blue Tit' look best? After reading Hillier's *Tree and Shrub Catalogue* from cover to cover and listing some 100 shrubs and trees which might be just what we wanted, we had to tour Hillier's' three gardens which then were extensive. This eliminated certain plants but, of course, added others. Visits over many years to stately homes and, of course, Kew, had provided me with notebooks full of desiderata, and

81

memories of plants loved in childhood gave a list of plants we had to have.

'Endless sheets of paper were covered with plans. Like pawns, plants were moved about to provide colour at every time of the year. Apart from the glory of the herbaceous bed in the summer, there was to be a blaze of colour in the autumn and the excitement of the spring aconites, snowdrops and daffodils, tulips and gentian.

'How far were the visions fulfilled? A soil analysis which showed that the acidity was extreme and needed three pounds of lime per square yard to bring it to neutrality eliminated some dreams. Blasting winds from north and south led, after many years of frustration, to giving up the tea-rose bed. Torrents of rain in the winter have found the gallica and alba roses standing for weeks in water. Poor 'Charles de Mills', 'Commandant Beaurepaire', 'Cardinal Richelieu' and the 'Queen of Denmark' have rebelled against this indignity and now this area plainly needs redeveloping. The wild flower meadow took only two years to prove that, on such a slope, cutting hay was only possible with a scythe and no one could be found to do it. It also showed that twitch, Yorkshire fog and cocksfoot grasses needed the winter nibbling of sheep to let the meadow flowers establish themselves. Flowery meadow had to change to more frequently cut grass. This had the consolation of showing off the shrubs but where are the wild flowers which were to be such a feature?

'The herbaceous border stands as it was planned with, of course, yearly small alterations. The rock garden immediately settled into the landscape. The excursion to Hillier's resulted in *Rosa* 'Céleste', 'Arthur Hillier', 'Hillieri', 'Penelope' and 'Cornelia', *Kolkwitzia amabilis* and *Berberis temolaica* giving endless delight. *Cedrus atlanticul glauca* after twelve years trying to gain a foothold in the Skiddaw slate has now shot up to give joy winter and summer. Joy but problems too, as I did not believe that, when I excavated a hole and drew out upright slivers of slate-like teeth, it would ever become so large in our lifetime that it would bar a path and threaten its neighbour.

'Other visions have materialized. The cherry Yukon stretches over favourite azaleas and the lovely copper beech hedge we planted. Blue poppies settled down to enjoy

TWO GNOMES IN A ROCK GARDEN ON CATBELLS

rain, wind and good drainage. *Rhododendron* 'Sappho' – white with a black blotch – has after twenty years of indifferent growth justified a childhood love and now burgeons every May.

'The *Acer palmatum ribesifolium*, with its neat upright habit and deeply cut leaves which turn yellow in the autumn and *Acer griseum*, known for its red peeling bark and flaming colour in October, have stood up to every gale and given deep satisfaction. *Cornus kousa* and *Kalmia latifolia* increase their beauty each year. *Rosa moyesii* 'Arthur Hillier' grows with abandon and its single, spectacular, deep rose-pink flowers flaunt their beauty on the bank.

'Grass-cutting problems led to extensive planting of junipers on the middle and lower slopes. These have taken over and are like wonderful waves of the sea and are great savers of labour. The autumn colours are there but fleeting. The glorious deciduous trees in the Cumbrian woods protect each other but single shrubs on a windswept hillside can display their colour for only a few days and the autumn crocus were abandoned as the winds tore them too cruelly.

'Wind is a great enemy. Devastating winds rock the shrubs to and fro, blow off the leaves and tear the flowers to shreds. The predominant wind is from the south so a shelter belt would cut off the sun and also the views which are the *raison d'être* of living here. Common sense says keep to the low-growing plants but the blue of delphiniums or the lure of the curious *Veratrum nigrum* puts that out of court.

'"Your house should be called 'Keep Moving'", said a friend. An apt title, as we endlessly moved plants about to get them in just the right position for their colour, height and shape. Getting older led to dabbling with the shrub and heather garden idea but, as long as catalogues keep coming, common sense disappears. Like drink, they lead to just another one, just one more plant that will need staking or pruning or feeding. As long as I can dream dreams and see visions I am tied to a life of spreading fertilizers, putting in birch twigs for plant supports and picking out thousands of weeds. Meantime, the wild rose burgeons on the roadside, perfect in its unordered beauty.'

Preserving the Dream

A c o r n   B a n k
T e m p l e   S o w e r b y

Acorn Bank is a very, very old garden and it's a garden with staying power. My first visit there I imagined would also be my last, because the garden was about to be closed.

When Dorothy Una Ratcliffe, poet, botanist and 'patroness of northern folk culture', gave the property to the National Trust in 1950, it came as a special trust without funding for the garden and the National Trust could not afford to subsidize it. The garden was run with contributions from an honesty box and operated at a loss (no connection I'm sure!), but it meant the Trust had no idea how much support there was for the garden. With an ever-increasing debt it was decided to close it, but Patrick Watson, the Managing Agent, and Nigel Sale, Regional Information Officer, decided to organize an appeal. The Trust agreed and £30,000 was raised over two years. The success of the appeal meant the garden could remain open.

It is the least flashy of the National Trust gardens in the area, without the nimbus of Beatrix Potter, a stunning view over Windermere or a surrealistic rock garden but, in a way, its charm is precisely that it has none of these things. Tucked away on the edge of the Lake District, it has an intimacy, stillness and rural quality you can absorb whether or not you're interested in the 250 varieties of herbs grown here.

Acorn Bank must always have had an aura of healing around it because it was originally a religious house and then a hospice for 300 years, set up in the thirteenth century by the Knights Templar. The house itself is currently leased to the Sue Ryder Foundation for the elderly and infirm. The garden's collection of medicinal and culinary herbs is the largest in northern England but, although herbs would have been used as a matter of course in medieval times, the ladies and gentlemen of the Sue Ryder home don't take their camomile tea from the garden.

When the National Trust took over the management of Acorn Bank in 1969, its garden adviser, Graham Stuart Thomas, was faced with a long, narrow, walled rect-angle. Fortunately, he had the foresight to anticipate a revival of interest in medicinal herbs not on show anywhere else and started the collection in what was an old vegetable garden. This unique feature probably saved the garden from oblivion.

The herb garden is divided into three long beds of sun-, semi-shade- and shade-loving herbs with a 'hot' wall against which apricots, peaches, and nectarines were grown 250 years ago. In those days it was cheaper than buying glass to employ an apprentice to stoke coal fires all night at the base of a flued wall to keep the warm air cir-culating in the wall cavity. During the night the frost was kept off the flowering trees by covering them with blankets.

This physic garden has been designed rather like that of a display collection for a teaching hospital, with aesthetics secondary to the welfare of the plants. The pleasing effects happen by accident but it has been noticed that plants which grow well together look good together. The old quince tree in the centre bed acts as a focal point, giving the garden character.

In the collection are enough plants to kill or cure you several times over. The National Trust publishes an excellent guide to the herbs at Acorn Bank, giving all their names and uses, but it does leave you feeling rather queasy; not recommended reading for hypochondriacs. The poisonous plants inspire the most awe and respect and the ones that particularly interest me are the witches' plants. These include belladonna, henbane, datura and stramonium, which are all poisonous as well as hallucinogenic. Witches would make up a concoction of these herbs, mixed with goose grease, and rub juice of euphorbia to induce blistering on their hands, then spread the mixture on the handles of their broom-sticks and set about their housework. And the more they swept, the more their hands be-came blistered and, as the blisters broke the skin, the ointment en-tered the bloodstream and they would begin hallucinating. They would all have had well-swept houses, I imagine, and the concoction

RESIDENTS ENJOY THE SPRING GARDEN

seems the forerunner to the modern housewife's gin and tranquillizers. It became known as 'flying ointment' and that is how witches came to 'fly' on broomsticks!

I was admiring the poisonous, half-hardy datura with its long white trumpets that is grown in the greenhouse and wondering what its effects would be. 'It has

(LEFT) THE HERB GARDEN; (RIGHT) URN FROM VERONA

an immediate effect,' said Chris Braithwaite, the head gardener, 'which gets worse! Not a thing you regret taking for long if you take enough of it.' The old greenhouse has been transformed into a conservatory. The original, Victorian greenhouse became very dilapidated and was beautifully restored and it now has a wider entrance to accommodate wheelchairs, necessary for the present inhabitants of Acorn Bank and any disabled visitors to enjoy its facilities.

In the orchard, everything comes in twos like Noah's Ark. There's a double border of old roses, a double hedge of clipped yew, a double row of *Prunus cerasus* 'Rhexii', varieties of apples in pairs, two quinces, two medlars and, just about to go in beyond the garden wall, a double avenue of Perry pears! The walls are festooned with roses and pears, with herbaceous and shrub borders at the foot. Along one wall is the beginnings of a lily border with just three species of lilies which I would like to see expand into a riot of different lilies. In spring, the orchard is carpeted with daffodils, wild tulips, fritillarias, the double white anemone, martagon lilies and, later, with colchicums and a wild flower called fox and cubs.

Beyond the garden gates at the back of the house is the wild garden planted by Dorothy Una Ratcliffe. She created a wild flower and bird reserve in the 1930s, planting 30,000 wild daffodils and specially grown wild flowers amongst the oaks of the 'acorn bank' which slopes down to a stream, the Crowdundle Back. She was also responsible for bringing in the picturesque fixtures – the gates, statues and vases from Verona which are scattered throughout the garden.

There's laconic humour to be found in this garden in the presence of Chris Braithwaite, who describes himself as a *laissez faire* gardener. He was sent to Sizergh on a government training scheme, under

CURTAINS OF VARIEGATED IVY

the impression he could spend a quiet year in the country before going back to city life in Newcastle or to working on an oil rig, but, 'It rather got hold and I didn't want to stop, so I didn't.' When a permanent job came up at Acorn Bank, he took it. 'I spent the first year in a total panic afraid I was going to kill everything and had no idea of what I was doing

at all! But Malcolm Hutcheson of Sizergh came up to help. Obviously I'd shown great promise as a student or they wouldn't have given me the job! I spent the first year observing and pulling out things that were obviously weeds and got myself a big book on herbs, *Mrs Grieve's Modern Herbal* which was written after the First World War and helped to treat the wounded of the Second. It has everything in it.' Since the appeal to save the garden, Chris has added another fifty herbs to the collection and he seems to have a personal relationship with each plant that grows in this two-and-a-half acre garden.

In order to maintain Acorn Bank on entrance money alone, the garden would need 40,000 visitors a year but this would be self-defeating as it would destroy the garden in the process. At present it draws about 15,000 visitors each year and the Trust hopes to attract a further 5,000, which the garden could cope with without damaging the grass paths and structure. The money raised by the appeal is currently being invested in a shop run by Chris's wife. Chris would also like the National Trust to start a herb nursery to put the garden on a 'sure footing' and secure the survival of the flying ointments.

G R A Y T H W A I T E   H A L L
H A W K S H E A D

M y l e s   S a n d y s

The Sandys family has links with Cumbria dating back to the time of King John in the thirteenth century. So, although I wasn't expecting to find the Lord of the Domain chopping down a dead cherry tree surrounded by Victorian shrubbery, neither did I expect to find this twentieth-century heir looking like an American movie star. As Myles Sandys led the way towards the house, he cut an incongruous figure against the Victorian Gothic mansion. But there was nothing green about this squire. In the five years since he took over Graythwaite Hall from his parents he has assumed total control, understanding the complexities of the estate, and sticking to his priorities. He is refreshingly outspoken.

'Mawson's [the original designer of the gardens] getting trendy,' Myles said. 'They've run out of ideas to write about so somebody's obviously said "Let's do Mawson" and it's finally put us on the map. We're on the wrong side of the lake. Everybody hoofed off to Brockhole and Stagshaw and all those, and we relied on passing trade. But now that they've discovered Mawson they actually come to see his creation, which is more than he would have ever done because when you lay out a garden you lay it out for the future and so you never see the finished product which is very sad in many ways. But I suppose you're equipped with imagination.'

It took the mysterious Thomas Mawson of Troutbeck, Windermere, four years to landscape the twelve acres of gardens around the Hall using the existing landscape which was made of rock formations and had only a very thin layer of soil. Even today, if you want to plant something you have to scratch a hole with a pick and fill it with soil. Mawson planted a woodland garden of choice rhododendrons, azaleas, spring-flowering trees and shrubs. There were only two formal parts: the rose garden, which was called the 'Ladies Walk' and had a sundial in the middle (now running half an hour out since one of Myles's small sons knocked the top off and it was concreted back on a cloudy day); and the Dutch garden with a box-edged parterre and symmetrically placed clipped yew. The garden today has retained the original layout and is planted with the traditional species of plants orginally grown – acid lovers which can stand up to wind and weather. The superb statues and sundial were made by Mawson's architect, Dan Gibson.

Gone, though, is the old tennis court which had pavilions and a big privet hedge around it. 'My grandparents lived in London in those days and they used to come up here in August and invite their friends over for tennis and you had to wear your whites. I remember, as a boy, tea being brought up to the tennis court by the butler and his staff on silver salvers, and teapots and cucumber sandwiches being lugged up there on a sunny August day. The two old gardeners, Sam and Jack Kellet, who tromped around in clogs and waistcoats, used to spend their life rolling it. It's now part of a field but it's a nice, flat area and one could always put one back.'

When Mawson was laying out the gardens, the work which would now be undertaken by a JCB was carried out by Irishmen with wheelbarrows. After that, the garden was maintained by seven gardeners with traditional tools and a lot of patience. Then the staff went down to two, and now it's one. But what a one!

A certain Charles Dudley Warner from America who is frequently in my thoughts when I'm out navvying in my garden said, 'What a man needs in gardening is a cast-iron back with a hinge in it.' Myles Sandys has done one better and hired himself a cast-iron man. Mark Kynman is a body builder and Myles reckons he must spend most of his salary on food because he eats 'something like 170 eggs, a dozen chickens and pounds and pounds of cod each week'.

Mark does look rather fearsome as you would expect of a primed juggernaut. I sat beside him on a rock somewhat gingerly, wondering which of the two was the hardest.

'Mr Sandys will come up with some ideas,' says Mark 'and we'll talk them over and decide.' He pointed to two mounds on the lawn. 'Those are lime tree stumps underneath there. We're going to remove them this year and replace them with two trees. Well, it's been going on now for six weeks trying to decide what trees we're actually going to plant but we've come to a decision. It's going to be a flowering malus so we get the flowers in the spring and the fruit in the autumn to get a bit of colour off the fruit. You have to choose a tree or a plant that you're 99 per cent sure is going to grow.'

Myles's parents moved up from London when he was ten, inheriting an estate that was in shambles. No one had lived there permanently for thirty years: Graythwaite Hall was nearly derelict, the fifty-three estate houses were in urgent need of attention and 2,500 acres of forest were poorly managed and producing no income. This was a call to battle and war was successfully fought. Borrowing 'like hell', Myles's father turned the estate around, commercializing the forest and utilizing all the assets on the estate to generate cash to repair the buildings. 'My parents will tell you that they spent their married life doing up houses.' The Hall took fifteen years to complete. 'The garden then was desperately closed in. The Victorians loved a claustrophic atmosphere – lots of dripping yew and laurel around the place right up to the house and everything

(ABOVE) GRAYTHWAITE HALL AMONGST THE RHODODENDRONS
(BELOW) DETAIL FROM THE DUTCH GARDEN IN SPRING

stank of mildew and moss. My parents cleared an enormous amount. They took out something like two or three hundred trees, mature trees, so that you could see through into the distance, into fields, and the air could get round it.'

The responsibility of taking over the estate intimidated Myles when he was younger and known as 'a very lively boy', but he was the only son. 'The sort of thing you're born to understand. You do it. And, yes, I wanted to do it. I lived in London for ten years and really hated it. I'm a country boy at heart. I'm very fond of the estate – it's been here a long time. My two boys are the first boys to be born here for two hundred years. We've got something now, we've built up a community – a lot of young people live here, married with small children. I think there are thirty children under twelve on the estate and there's a good Christmas party. I hope my two boys will maintain interest and crack on. Edward shows all the right signs and he's interested in wild life, outdoors, trees, animals – it's a start, isn't it? I'll explain all about Inland Revenue and planning permission later.'

His father first opened the garden to the public partly to cover the cost of running it but also because it's a listed garden. 'It's a garden of immense interest to gardeners and I think unless you open to the public it won't be seen and interest will wane. One day, I might seriously need some help with the house or garden and if people have never heard of it or are not interested in it I am really not going to get much help from anybody. It's a historical garden and a historical house. People come back year after year. In fact, they notice things that I don't. They say "Oh, I'm so glad you've replaced that awful thing with something new," and this is quite encouraging. People understand what it costs and the time it takes to maintain a garden like this.' Over 2,500 people visit each year which is an achievement as the garden is only open for the months of April, May and June and is somewhat off the beaten track.

The original Myles Sandys was known as the 'Colonel with the cash' which he spent freely on Graythwaite Hall. A hundred years later his namesake has not only to think about

WROUGHT IRON GATES BY DAN GIBSON

making a go of the estate but also to show sensitivity to the landscape. And so, all the conifer plantations are surrounded by broad-leaved woods and he is planting thousands of others. 'You couldn't work for a better boss,' said the bionic gardener of this modern improvement to the Lord of the Domain.

S I Z E R G H   C A S T L E
K E N D A L

'Now this,' said Malcolm Hutcheson, the head gardener, as we both looked up a *Cypress lawsonii* so high we couldn't see the top of it, 'is supposed to be a dwarf conifer.'

We were standing in the rock garden for which Sizergh has been famous since 1927, but in which no gnome would now feel at home as there is rather less rock visible now and rather more garden. And although forty feet is perhaps a little high for a dwarf conifer, it is sixty years since it was planted. It has grown and grown 'for the simple reason', writes Graham Stuart Thomas, the National Trust's garden adviser, 'that there was little else for it to do!'

We made our way through the bottom of the rock garden, the bare patches here and there reflecting the purge on Malcolm's current nightmare, a pernicious weed with the deceptively sweet name of Mare's Tail which has to be completely killed before he can carry out his plan to replant with choice plants. We made our way up the other side, around a weeping dwarf hemlock, fifteen feet wide, which had overgrown two paths and has to be constantly pruned to allow anyone through.

The view from the top of the rock garden looking down towards the castle is impressive, particularly considering it was carved out of an orchard, each piece of native limestone brought in and positioned by a team of horses with eight men. Watercourses were made to run through the garden, linking the natural pond above with the stream below, which was enlarged into a small lake with an island.

The rock garden was commissioned by Lord and Lady Strickland at a time when rock gardens were at the height of fashion. It was designed by Waring, a local architect, and executed by T. R. Hayes of Ambleside. Into it went ferns, maples, berberis and acer seedlings from Japan with rare and unusual colours, local rock plants and dwarf pines which were originally only the size of a man's fist but are now full grown.

During the war years the rock garden became overgrown with berberis and the water courses became blocked and dried out. When the Strickland family gave the castle and gardens to the National Trust in 1955, work began on clearing the watercourses and restoring the rock garden. It soon became apparent that nearly an acre had been buried under grass and shrubs.

Restoring an overgrown garden inevitably presents difficulties. 'We've got to remove these big specimens and get the feeling of a rock garden, leaving the lovely weep-

'Swan Lake' at the foot of the Castle

ing forms. We're not going to desecrate the thing, obviously.' The Strickland family still live at Sizergh and are very attached to the large eccentric specimens, remembering when they were first planted and they must seem like old family pets. So, when a big specimen is removed to make room for a younger one, it's an important decision. The National Trust has to think about what the garden is going to look like for the general public in fifty years and is less sentimental in its approach.

Malcolm is the National Trust's regional head gardener and, as well as being a knowledgeable gardener, diplomat, natural historian and an exceedingly kind man, he's physically suited to his job. A lanky six-footer with big feet, he's adept at dealing with the Sizergh-sized 'dwarf' conifer and settling the *Gentiana acaulis* border when it heaves with frost. Because Sizergh is an important National Trust property, visitors expect it to look good from the time it first opens its gates at Easter, and this creates an enormous pressure on Malcolm. 'It really is hard work to get everything ready for spring. The winters are long, the lads go home at four when it gets dark. You want your grass in good order for the public but you can't touch it before the beginning of April. It's all right people saying, "You must get scarifying and fertilizing," but here it's either pouring with rain or frozen solid.

ROCK GARDEN OF ACERS AND FERNS

THE HERBACEOUS BORDER, MIDSUMMER

'If you go to Cornwall in March, the magnolias are flowering. South-west gardeners don't know they're lucky. The season is two months shorter here, so all the work – the rock garden with its Mare's Tail, lawns and propagating – has to be condensed into eight weeks and we're understaffed as it is. More money is spent on the garden than on anything else and even that is not enough.' So the resourceful Malcolm, who loves propagating, has instigated the Great Sizergh Plant Sale each May, the profits of which give the garden an extra boost.

Yet, strangely enough, the wet climate and the shortage of staff have influenced the development of two of the most interesting features of the garden: the fern collection and the wildflower bank.

The 1865 edition of a small leather book entitled *Ferns of the English Lake Country* by W. J. Linton has the following first paragraph:

The English Lake Country might not inappropriately be called The Land of Ferns, for there is no other part of the kingdom, perhaps, which affords greater facilities for their propagation and growth. The climate and soil are peculiarly adapted to their luxuriant development. . . Of the 43 species of true ferns indigenous to Great Britain, 35 are found in the Lake Country.

Collecting ferns was a Victorian craze much prized by the Wordsworths and John Ruskin. Like all crazes, it predictably went out of fashion and most of the big fern collections disappeared. Luckily, Hayes the nurserymen were able to salvage one of these collections and planted it in Sizergh's rock garden. When the National Trust took over, Graham Stuart Thomas in his infinite wisdom recognized its value and the collection has grown to become part of the National Fern Collection of Britain. Malcolm, who didn't know one fern from another when he first came, is now a fern addict and adds to it all the time. Recently, the Japanese painted ferns with pink and silver fronds have been planted to encourage the public's revival of interest.

Being a natural historian, Malcolm likes to let things run semi-wild – hence the willow gentian which is allowed to seed itself freely in the rock garden and has led to the second popular feature at Sizergh – the wildflower bank. This has developed partly from his interest in wildflowers and natural flora and partly, it is admitted, from a shortage of staff. Cumberland and Westmorland have the richest source of botanical flora in the country because it's a limestone region. There is a bony, almost soil-less, limestone bank with a marvellous collection of wildflowers which natural history groups come to study. There are eighty butterfly orchids in June, the little adders-tongue fern, a green-veined orchid and so on. The adders-tongue fern is reputed to be rare in Cumbria and so Sizergh counted them this spring. After noting 2,000, everyone gave up. Orchid seeds are like particles of dust which can travel hundreds of miles on a thunder system from as far away as Bedfordshire and can take seven years to produce a flower. So we have no idea how many others are lying there incubating.

This sort of collection happens only through proper management of the turf. Daffodils flower on the bank in the spring and the grass used to be cut in June and kept mown all summer. But 'my thought on that', says Malcolm, 'was to leave it be and let them seed and flower – and take the hay off later.' And, anyway, 'Why should we be wearing out our mowers and our staff cutting grass that doesn't need cutting?' By starving the big grasses and letting the little ones grow, it has also allowed the native flora to come up alongside.

Sizergh has always had a mystique about it. Its 1360 pele tower covered with Boston ivy rises above a glass lake with swans. It is flanked by immaculately kept lawns, shrub and herbaceous borders, which give it a romantic atmosphere. The eccentric rock garden gives it character. The wildflower bank adds natural beauty. Sizergh is a great testament to Malcolm's practical and imaginative approach, which has kept it as a great visual treat as well as preserving in its wildflowers and ferns the Lakeland gardening tradition.

H I L L   T O P ,   S A W R E Y

B e a t r i x   P o t t e r

Hill Top was the kind of garden Beatrix Potter had wanted all her life and it finally materialized when she was forty-six. She bought it with money she had earned herself, between the four walls of the Victorian household in which she was brought up. And once she had it, she never relinquished it.

Her parents had made their fortunes from the textile mills in Lancashire but had made their lives in London. Beatrix and her brother Bertram felt the north call them back from an early age and both of them chose to live there as painters and farmers and died there. When Beatrix was a child her grandmother told her stories about Abraham Compton, Beatrix's great-grandfather, a prosperous Lancashire mill owner, noted for his radical politics and his curious habit of picking snails off a wall and eating them alive! He had bought a farm in the Lake District where he and his thirteen children spent summer holidays and went on to buy more, a pattern Beatrix was later to repeat. Her grandmother had a 'dreamlike recollection of driving with her father in a gig across Lancaster Sands to buy one of these farms as the moon was rising and the tide coming in rapidly and she was sitting beside him holding the bag of gold and wishing he'd go faster.' Beatrix's life held many parallels with her great-grandfather's. His individuality, indifference to public opinion and fascination with farms all found their way into her own life and her links with the Lake District were made at a very early age.

Neither of her parents were gardeners and her childhood garden in Kensington, London, has been described as a daisy lawn, two trees and a narrow border; no doubt as narrow as her parents were. So when she first discovered the 'cottage' garden it immediately caught her imagination. Family holidays were spent in Perthshire, where Beatrix first saw among rickyards and cottages the 'farmhouse' garden where herbs, vegetables and annuals grow mixed together; unplanned, asymmetrical and unpretentious. This, together with her uncle's cottage garden, Gwaynygog, in Wales, which she described as 'the prettiest kind of garden where bright old-fashioned flowers grow among the currant bushes' became the basis of her garden at Hill Top in Cumbria. The vegetable garden delighted her as did the paraphernalia of the kitchen garden – potting sheds, cold frames, clay pots, wooden wicket gates, well-worn gardening tools, and scarecrows. These were all important elements in the setting for her first book *Peter Rabbit* in Mr McGregor's garden, the most famous garden in England.

It was the simplicity and earthiness of rural life which appealed to Beatrix, probably idealized because it was so different from her upbringing. She and her brother, Bertram, were allowed few friends but had developed a great affinity to animals in the study, care, dissection and drawing of them. By the time Bertram went away to school, they had spent many years in the upstairs nursery botanizing and drawing. Beatrix was then left alone to concentrate solely on her work which she might not have done if she had lived in a social whirl, married young and put away her paintbrushes for baby booties. A proposal of marriage did finally come her way in a Trojan horse when she was an established children's author in the guise of her publisher, Norman Warne. In the same year, 1905, she bought Hill Top Farm as an 'investment' but, sadly, shortly after the proposal Norman died suddenly. 'I thought my story had come right,' she wrote to Norman's sister Millie, 'after all that patience and waiting.'

After the funeral it was to Hill Top Beatrix went with her shattered dream – having lost her best friend, her freedom and the prospect of any children. Beatrix liked children because she could share her own childish fantasies with them. 'I have just made stories to please myself because I never grew up!' she wrote in a letter. All the same she perhaps may have wondered if her stories were destined always to be read to other people's children. Her cousin Ulla Parker described Beatrix's reaction when she visited her at Hill Top with her newborn baby: Beatrix looked at the baby and said, 'A baby here at last – something I did always so long for.'

Gardening is nurturing of a different kind. Beatrix had to make a new beginning and it started with her garden, her first garden. Writing to Millie she said, 'My news is all gardening at present, and supplies. I went to see an old lady at Windermere and impudently took a large basket and trowel with me. She had the most untidy overgrown garden I ever saw. I got nice things in handfuls without any shame, amongst others a bundle of violet suckers. I am going to set some of them in the orchard . . . Mrs Satterthwaite says stolen plants always grow. I stole some ''honesty'' yesterday, it was put to be burnt in a heap of garden refuse! I have had something out of nearly every garden in the village.' Then, always practical: 'I think I shall attack the County Council about manure. I am entitled to all the road sweepings along my piece, and their old man is using it to fill up holes.'

Beatrix didn't live at Hill Top full-time, as she was still based with her parents, and her time there became like a love affair of stolen moments. In those years, until she finally married, she produced thirteen little books, three of which used her own garden

BORDER FROM 'THE TALE OF TOM KITTEN',
LEADING TO HILLTOP

for their setting – whilst a fourth drew upon a garden in the village.

Jemima Puddleduck lays her eggs in the rhubarb patch in the vegetable garden and picks sage and onion for the Gentleman with Sandy Whiskers in the long wide border ('The stupid clot!' says the present lady in the Hill Top shop vehemently). This is actually the same border painted so prettily in the *Tale of Tom Kitten*.

Beatrix gardened as she painted, with an exquisite eye for colour and every detail. Her characters all dressed beautifully in fine embroidered clothes and pretty patterns with the exception of Mr McGregor, who dressed more like her. Beatrix was famous for the ankle-length tweed suit she wore, with black clogs to keep her feet dry. She was eccentric in her choice of hats which have been variously described as a knitted bonnet, a tea cosy, a rhubarb leaf, an old felt or straw hat with pieces of elastic or tape tied under her chin. Sometimes she had a piece of sacking over her shoulders, to keep off the rain, and she was followed about the village by her pet pig who answered to the name of Sally. One person who knew her said, 'She didn't care about dress and she didn't seem to care much for anybody who cared about dress.' This idea of dressing for show is marvellously satirized in *The Tale of Tom Kitten* which is set at Hill Top and makes a complete mockery of forcing children into 'elegant uncomfortable clothes' – how incongruous and impractical they are in a garden.

The frontispiece to this book reveals Beatrix's spring garden of daffodils, stems of bleeding heart, dianthus in bud, lobelia and, trained along the rose trellis, an espalier of apple blossom. The pictures in *The Tale of Tom Kitten* were painted at different times during the year – later in the book we jump to June with a clematis-clad porch and, on another page, snapdragons, cabbage roses, pansies, dianthus, peony and iris.

In the *Sequel to the Fairy Caravan*, which was never published, Beatrix describes her own porch: 'First there is the porch made of great slabs of Brathay slate, on either side a slate six foot high, with two smaller slates for the roof, and honeysuckle and cabbage roses hanging over. The flowers love the house, they try to come in! The golden-flowered great St John's wort pushes up between the flags in the porch; it has peeped up between the skirting and the flags inside the porch place before now. And the old lilac bush that blew down had its roots under the parlour floor, when they lifted the boards. Houseleek grows on the window sills and ledges; wisteria climbs the wall, clematis chokes the spout's casings. Wallflowers and cabbage roses in season; rosemary and blue gentian, and earliest to flower the red Japanese quince – but nothing more sweet than the old pink cabbage rose, that peeps in at the small-paned windows.'

When Beatrix Potter did eventually marry, it was to a local solicitor, William Heelis, at the age of fifty-three. Although she lived her married life at the neighbouring Castle Farm, she kept Hill Top on where she squirrelled away mementoes and

memories of her artistically creative life. She loved both her Cumbrian homes, pottering about like Mrs Tiggywinkle and keeping everything clean and well-ordered.

Hill Top, left to the National Trust along with her fourteen farms when she died in 1943, became a museum even in her own lifetime. Beatrix painted there and entertained there. So many people came to see her that she kept a rabbit hutch with a rabbit in it so visiting children would not be disappointed in their search for Peter. In the same tradition, the ladies who now run the Hill Top shop have put an egg in Jemima Puddle-duck's rhubarb patch.

LANDSCAPE WHERE BEATRIX POTTER'S ASHES
ARE SCATTERED

D O V E   C O T T A G E
G R A S M E R E

William   and   Dorothy
Wordsworth

William Wordsworth lived the first twenty years of his life in the Lake District and spent the next ten wandering through England and France with only one wish – to return to Grasmere. And so, in 1799, Wordsworth came on a walking holiday with his friend Samuel Taylor Coleridge with the idea of building a house on the shores of Grasmere Lake. But by the time the holiday was over, he had instead rented a small whitewashed cottage, an old inn called the 'Dove and Olive Bough', which we know today as Dove Cottage. Wordsworth denounced whitewashed cottages in the Lake District – which didn't stop him moving into one – saying they pulled your eye down from the horizon, were too conspicuous and a blot on the landscape. Their remedy for Dove Cottage was to smother the walls with honeysuckle, roses and jasmine and, while they were waiting for these to grow, they planted scarlet runner beans which grew right up to the eaves of the house. Wordsworth also planted two yew trees outside his front garden to cut out the 'glare of the white house for people coming down the road'.

A year after they moved in, Dorothy wrote, 'We are daily more delighted with Grasmere . . . we have a boat upon the lake and a small orchard and smaller garden which as it is the work of our own hands we regard with pride and partiality.'

George Kirkby has been Chief Guide at Dove Cottage for eighteen years and gardener for twenty-one and there's nothing he doesn't know about this most celebrated of spots. William and Dorothy Wordsworth did not have a typical cottage garden – theirs was a garden of subtlety and detail. Like Ruskin, Wordsworth hated 'exotics' and was much influenced by his many travel books on Japan, giving the garden its Japanese atmosphere. 'Wordsworth was a good gardener,' says George, 'Dorothy was a good gardener but not a great horticulturalist. She gardened instinctively. I think a lot of her gardening skill came from observation. If you see primroses growing on a bank in dappled shade and you do the same you don't go wrong and that's what she did.'

The Wordsworths' 'domestic ship of mountain ground' was divided into the flower garden and beyond, where the museum now stands, the orchard garden 'which is nineteenth century for an allotment. We think of an orchard as trees but they didn't. It was

THE ROSE 'PRELUDE' ADORNS A POET'S SHRINE

traditional to keep the orchard garden well away from the house so that if you kept hens or geese they didn't paddle in and paddle it down and, even today, there are one or two farms in Grasmere whose kitchen gardens are half a mile from the house.'

Everyone worked in the orchard garden, all activities noted by Dorothy in her journals. Molly Fisher, the daily cleaner who lived next door, was sent out to plant potatoes, William stuck peas, Dorothy transplanted radishes. Hardly a day goes by in the season where there isn't some reference to the preparing, planting, weeding, hoeing and harvesting of their vegetables. This was an early Romantic idea of living the 'good life', being self-sufficient and enjoying a simple, rural and wholesome existence. Yeats talks of his nine rows of beans but Wordsworth actually grew them. Wordsworth was quite practical in the garden and built a moss hut.

John Fisher built a drystone wall to make a terraced platform for Wordsworth to walk up and down while composing poetry. Just above the terrace in the top corner of the garden they built an Indian bower out of green timber – 'Our own contrivance – Building without Peer!' with a wonderful view over the lake and fells. And there William and Dorothy sat many an evening, whatever the weather, absorbing a view described by Dorothy in autumn as 'all colours melting into each other'.

The garden was hedged with local hazel, sycamore, rowan and hollies. William

A 'SHADY NOOK' OF MOSS AND FERN

was particularly fond of hollies and he is reported to have carried a pocketful of holly berries around with him as an old man, planting them all over the county. Roses, sunflowers, yellow and white turk's cap lilies, honeysuckle under the yew tree, pansies and Michaelmas daisies comprised the flowery side to the garden, but the real favourites were wildflowers, ferns, mosses and lichens. Dorothy had a basket especially for gathering mosses which she would plant alongside ferns, favouring the Royal Fern – so big you can almost sit under it. They would have learned from the locals that ferns make wonderful compost when cut green and mixed in with kitchen waste. And after the ferns had died down they would have seen that the wood sorrel had made its home there, with green leaves all winter and flowers in the spring, and dog's tooth violets growing through moss and all around. Wordsworth called Dorothy 'his eyes and ears', not suprisingly as he lived with someone who noted down in her Journal the precise time and day she observed the tiny sorrel leaves unfolding.

Dorothy gathered wildflowers wherever she went and many wildflowers found their way into the Dove Cottage garden – pimpernel, periwinkle, lichens, ragged robin, speedwell, stitchwort, *Anemone nemerosa*, snowdrops, foxgloves, Lenten lilies (wild daffodils). It is interesting that even in those days they were conservation-conscious. In her Journal, Dorothy writes of rowing to Loughrigg fell in July to 'visit the white foxglove' and again in late August she notes, 'walked around two lakes and gathered white fox-

104

glove seeds'. The white foxglove had been rare and she had honoured it with a special second visit, waiting patiently meantime for the seeds to ripen. She loved primroses, writing 'my garden is in its full primrose glory', and on one of her excursions dug a primrose out of the top of a rock, got half-way home, felt guilty, and returned to replant it. William also desisted digging up the rare moss campion and attacked insensitive collectors as people who would 'botanize on their mothers' graves'.

The Dove Cottage era was the most creative period in Wordsworth's life. Much of his happiness was bound up with his garden. He wrote 'The Green Linnet', 'To the Daisy', 'The Recluse', 'The Sparrow's Nest' ('And in this bush our sparrow built her nest of which I sang one song that will not die') and 'A Farewell' specifically about it. When he was in the garden, he always got his priorities right. 'One day,' says George, 'he was composing his ode on "Intimations of Immortality" when a farmer came with a load of dung and William went to work in the garden. What Emerson calls "the high watermark of English literature" was set aside while William went and spread the dung.' All things are relative.

These quiet, happy days ended with William's marriage to Mary Hutchinson. When William and Dorothy left Dove Cottage for William's Yorkshire wedding and a trip to France, it was to his garden that he wrote 'A Farewell', blessing it with the gardener's prayer, 'Sunshine and shower be with you, bud and bell'.

After their return, William and Mary produced three children in quick succession and, as the saying goes, 'there is no more sombre enemy to poetry than a baby crying in the night'. They outgrew Dove Cottage and moved to a bigger house leaving Dove Cottage in the care of his friend de Quincey. Dove Cottage had meant everything to William and Dorothy but, unfortunately, de Quincey's idea of gardening was not Wordsworth's. He was outraged to find de Quincey had cut down his outside hedge and replaced it with a stone wall, cut down many of his trees and plants to let more light into the orchard garden, and demolished his precious moss hut!

> Though nothing can bring back the hour
> Of splendour in the grass, of glory in the flower;
> We will grieve not, rather find
> Strength in what remains behind.

In Dorothy's Journal, if a tourist went by, it was worthy of comment: 'A coronetted landau went by when we were sitting up on the sodded wall. The ladies [evidently tourists] turned an eye of interest upon our little garden and cottage.' Today, 80,000 pairs of eyes devour the place each year. The last time I was at Dove Cottage, the Minister of the Arts' sleek limousine was parked outside. All things are relative, indeed.

R Y D A L   M O U N T
R Y D A L

William   and   Mary   and
Dorothy   Wordsworth

The life that William and Dorothy Wordsworth had led at Dove Cottage was quite unusual for people of their class and social standing, their behaviour eccentric to say the least – even by today's standards. Says George Kirkby, guide at Dove Cottage: 'If you were to walk up that hill today and there was a man and woman lying in a gutter side by side saying to each other, "This is what it must be like to be dead, next to our friends with the birds singing," you'd be across the road out of the way as quickly as possible.'

People in those days thought them very strange but marriage, in William and Dorothy's life, brought propriety. By the time Wordsworth moved into Rydal Mount, he had left his ideal of 'perfect democracy of agriculturalists and shepherds' to become a member of the establishment. He took on a job that brought him the equivalent of £25,000 per year and was teased by Coleridge's son, Hartley, who said, 'How great is William the Poet and how dull and boring is William Wordsworth, the squire, and Distributor of Stamps.'

The 'visionary gleam' which had lit up Wordsworth's best work was now sporadic. He wrote, 'I see in glimpses now and then, at times I see no more.' He looked for consolation in politics – as contradictory as his choice of houses – his daughter Dora noting, 'For every hour my father gives to poetry he gives twenty to politics.' He also took up landscape gardening, writing to Colonel Beaumont, whose garden at Colerton he had landscaped, that he had been gifted in three areas: poetry, art criticism and landscape gardening.

Rydal Mount had been an old farmhouse backed by fells and was ideally situated with views of Rydal and Windermere and the fells beyond. In front of the house is a little knoll, an old Norse post, called the Mount. It is here that Wordsworth composed his Evening Ode, imagining he saw the steps to paradise rising into the clouds in the distance. The family took tea there and on his seventy-fourth birthday the whole mount was alive with 300 children playing in their prettiest frocks. This was arranged at the instigation of Isabella Fenwick, whom he had met at sixty. She became his amanuensis and he detailed to her all the sources and places that inspired his poetry. In a way, Isa-

RYDAL MOUNT IN MAY

bella took Dorothy's place. William had always needed the adulation of a woman and Dorothy had become very ill with gallstones which led to arteriosclerosis and eventually affected her mind. Dorothy outlived William by five years, but was for all intents and purposes lost to him for the last twenty years of his life.

Although Dorothy's involvement with the garden at Rydal Mount was not so intense as it had been at Dove Cottage, William came into his own here, putting into practice all his theories about preserving harmony in the landscape. The layout of this garden was the same as at Dove Cottage – an orchard, a terrace (not six feet long but 250), and a sloping lawn that led to a kitchen garden. At the end of his 250-foot terrace, William built a summerhouse of Lakeland stone with a pebbled floor and a pine-coned interior. Then he made another terrace called the Far Terrace where he bellowed out his poetry and was described by the head gardener's boy like this: 'He was out upon the grass walk and would set his head a bit forward and put his hands behind his back. And he would start a bumming, and it was bum, bum, stop; then bum, bum, bum, right down till the other end and then he'd sit down and get a bit of paper out and write a bit. I suppose the bumming helped him out a bit.

'I often ask myself,' he wrote, 'what will become of Rydal Mount after our day. Strangely do the tastes of men differ, according to their employment and habits of life. "What a nice wall would that be", said a labouring man to me the other day, "if all that

107

rubbish was cleared off.'' The ''rubbish'' was some of the most beautiful mosses and lichens and ferns and other wild growths as could possibly be seen. Defend us from the tyranny of trimness and neatness showing itself in this way!'

Today, the mosses and ferns are still there as is his greatest legacy, in my view, the trees he planted. Scots pine, lime, a magnificent cut-leaf beech, a copper beech, birches, hollies, oak, maples and magnolia give the garden its serene and subtle beauty.

Yet the vision of the Wordsworths I am left with as I visit the garden is not that of William striding up and down the terrace, but of Dorothy being pushed around the garden in her bathchair, her mind gone, capable only of reciting reams and reams of William's poetry. She may have remembered a poem she herself wrote in 1834, the year before her mind went completely, commemorating her first walk alone after she and William had arrived in their chosen vale, thirty-five years before.

My youthful wishes all fulfill'd
Wishes matured by thoughtful choice,
I stood an Inmate of this Vale
How could I but rejoice?

L I N G H O L M   G A R D E N S

K E S W I C K

V i s c o u n t   a n d   V i s c o u n t e s s   R o c h d a l e

Lingholm is a garden of first loves and, like all first loves, remains special for ever. It was here that I swooned under my first *Rhododendron* 'Loderi', reeled under the glittering leaves of a soaring backlit beech, and was enchanted by a grove of blue Himalayan poppies growing wild in a clearing in the woodland garden. These are things the English find quite normal but for somebody like me, fresh from the untamed woods of New England, it was very exotic.

Situated on the shores of Derwentwater across the lake from where I live, Lingholm is the closest to me of all the gardens in this book. In March, when the frogs begin croaking at night in the pond outside my window with the promise of spring, the first place I visit is Lingholm. Inside the Victorian greenhouses it is lovely and warm, the air filled with the musky smell of fresh earth and *Rhododendron* 'Fragrantissimum' flowering. There are yellow cystisus, primroses, seedlings and green buds on the vines and everything is clean, bright and well-ordered. Sid Harrison, head gardener for thirty years, used to stand there pricking out faithful to his post. He was a typical Yorkshireman, not saying very much but smiling quietly and then sending me home with the most glorious rose for my conservatory or baby geraniums that grow like triffids. He has since retired and Mike Swift has taken over with the same Midas touch.

The atmosphere of Lingholm kindled my passion for gardens and the gardening bug is a contagious one. I caught mine from Lingholm, the creator of Lingholm caught his from the creator of Muncaster Castle. Colonel George Kemp (later Lord Rochdale) bought Lingholm in 1900, the house having been built in the 1870s for a Colonel Greenall by Waterhouse. In the late 1890s the house had changed hands and was often let for the summer months, and certainly for two or three years to Beatrix Potter's family, where the young Beatrix was to immortalize the place in her book *Squirrel Nutkin*. The story begins in the Woodland of Lingholm which she calls Nutkin's Wood, and even after the characters row across to Owl's Island (really St Herbert's Island), the setting is still based on Lingholm's woods. Writing to her publisher about Mr McGregor's garden in 1942, she says, 'If the vegetable garden and wicket gate were anywhere it was at Lingholm; but it would be vain to look for it there, as a firm of landscape gardeners did

away with it . . .'

Colonel Kemp built the terraces at the front of the house on whose steps heather
has been allowed to spread, leaving only a narrow path in the middle. It provides a
subtle and interesting effect and an attractive solution to accommodating heather in a
garden. He also built a star-shaped garden and later a water garden designed by
Symons Jenne, both of which have disappeared as it proved impossible to maintain
them during the Second World War and during the period of economic stringency of
the post-war years. But it was his great friend, Sir John Ramsden, of Muncaster Castle,
who in the 1920s inspired Colonel Kemp's enthusiasm for rhododendrons and gave him
a generous supply of seedlings which were planted in Squirrel Nutkin's wood. This is
how the collection started and it is the main feature of the garden today.

There has been a concerted effort to keep the garden looking as natural as possible.
Indeed among the wild dramatic fells of the Borrowdale Valley, a formal garden would
look ridiculous. Lingholm is surrounded by fells which have strong shapes of their own.
There's Catbells, with her long and bony spine which brings to mind a great old dino-
saur in the back garden, and Skiddaw, our version of Mount Olympus with his twin
peaks grandly presiding over the valley, and then there's Causey Pike with her dis-
tinctively maternal aspect. Across the lake are Walla and Falcon crags which Beatrix
Potter depicted in *Squirrel Nutkin*, a familiar scene to many parents. And, right in the
middle of it all, is Lingholm – the jewel in the crown.

Even the most natural-looking gardens have surprisingly unnatural beginnings.
Records show that at the end of the eighteenth century there were no forest trees on this
side of the lake – probably, surmises the present Lord Rochdale, because there would
have been scrub oak cut for smelting the copper that came up Newlands Valley. But in
the nineteenth century Lord William Gordon, who lived about a mile from Lingholm in
Derwent Bay House, planted the whole shore with trees and wouldn't allow any to be
cut down. This policy was carried on by his descendant, Major-General Sir John
Woodford – a veteran of Waterloo, and this created the ideal conditions for the cultiva-
tion of the rhododendron and other acid-loving plants. Indeed, the plantsman Roy
Lancaster is on record as saying Lingholm is the prefect re-creation of the rhododendron's natural habitat in the Himalayas!

The present Lord Rochdale grew up in Rochdale in Lancashire but spent the holidays at the family home at Lingholm. After the Second World War and his father's
death he became responsible for the garden. He was not quite forty at the time he
moved to Lingholm and already had a number of other commitments. He was a
governor of the BBC, Chairman of the Cotton Board, involved in several government
inquiries and, of course, a new member of the House of Lords, in which he played an

CAUSEY PIKE'S 'MATERNAL ASPECT'!

DEEP IN THE WOODLAND GARDEN

active role.

Initially, he had to cut down the maintenance of the garden in order to make it more manageable. However, he, Lady Rochdale, Sid Harrison and now Mike Swift with a small staff have developed the garden over the years, extending the season and range of plants but always keeping it as natural-looking as possible, and a peaceful refuge from a very busy life. 'I do a lot of work in the garden myself, say at the weekends, which is nice. There's no doubt that a garden, large or small, has a very soothing effect on one. It's the colour. You can see the result of your own work and ideas. It's a lovely thing to be able to have and to invite one's friends to enjoy too. Personally, I like feeling that the effort one puts into it is appreciated by many more people than just oneself and one's own friends,' Lord Rochdale says.

This kind of generous thinking led Lord and Lady Rochdale to open Lingholm Gardens to the public. It was already open one or two days a year under the National Gardens Scheme. In fact, it had been one of the first gardens to open on this basis when the scheme first started sixty-five years ago. And recently, to celebrate this anniversary, Lingholm was presented with a commemorative tree, and Sid Harrison was singled out to receive a medal for the remarkable job he has done with the garden. Mike Swift now

JAPANESE MAPLE, RH. 'CYNTHIA' AND WALLA CRAG

carries the torch but the mission is the same: 'To create and maintain an atmosphere of beauty, of nature and of peace. So many people come and say how peaceful it all is here.'

To many people, this garden will always be synonymous with Beatrix Potter and her naughty red squirrel. Lady Rochdale was looking out of the window one day and saw a party of Japanese arrive with little models of many Potter characters. They arranged them on the lawn, ran back to photograph them and then picked them up and took them off to the next location on their tour. Beatrix Potter's work is extremely popular in Japan and all her books have been translated into Japanese. And I, for one, can't go into the sloping vegetable garden without remembering it as it was ten years ago, before today's leylandii hedges and propagating tunnels bisected it. Then I found a similar sloping vegetable garden but with a wicket gate and woods behind, just like Mr McGregor's garden.

To most people, this is a garden where the fell is perfectly wedded to the flower. And every spring, when the plants I have from Lingholm start blooming in my conservatory, I have to revisit it just in case there's some new and exciting plant Mike Swift has propagated over the winter. There always is.

113

M U N C A S T E R   C A S T L E
R A V E N G L A S S

P a t r i c k   G o r d o n - D u f f
P e n n i n g t o n

I t was at Muncaster Castle that I saw my first davidia in bloom 'flapping its great white handkerchiefs' on a blustery May day. I had never seen anything so beautiful and came away remembering nothing of the rhododendrons. This was to change when I returned to photograph the gardens for this book, and change even more drastically when I met Patrick Gordon-Duff Pennington.

Poet, farmer, gardener, raconteur, rebel, and *homme extraordinaire*, he is called 'Patrick of the Hills'. His real home is in the Scottish Highlands where his family has a large estate. When Muncaster passed on to Phyllida, his wife, they decided that the only way to maintain it properly was to live there. It's no secret that after six years his heart and soul still blow freely in the wilderness of the Scottish hills.

Muncaster has belonged to Phyllida's family since 1200. The Castle was originally built as a pele tower 300 feet up Muncaster Fell and has magnificent views over Eskdale and the central Lake District fells. It's a lovely garden to look out from as well as into.

I think it has always been a dream garden. Reading a description of it by a person called 'Wanderer' in the 1905 issue of *The Journal of Horticulture and Home Farmer* during the reign of the last Lord Muncaster it sounded absolutely delectable. Although it had many shrubs and some very fine trees, it was primarily a rose garden. 'Thousands of hybrid and tea roses grew in different parts of the grounds as well as having a well-stocked rosery growing on a slope next to a Chinese garden with curiously shaped beds.'

Inside the walled garden (then the kitchen garden and now the nursery garden), were fruit houses of peaches and nectarines, an early and late vinery, a fernery and large and low-roofed hot houses with bougainvillea, clerodendron, and in the flowering house lapageria hung from the roof. 'Wanderer' noted that Mr Shaw, the head gardener, 'has been here a number of years and is a very industrious man and I am pleased to see he has lived to see many great results from his labours.' What he would have made of the next incumbent changing the garden from roses to rhododendrons is anyone's guess, as the poet O'Shaughnessy wrote, 'For each age is a dream that is

SWEEPING VIEW ACROSS THE GHYLL

dying, or one that is coming to birth.'

Lord Muncaster died without an heir and Muncaster passed to Phyllida's grand-father, Sir John Ramsden, with the proviso that his second son changed his name to Pennington. Sir John Ramsden was a rhododendron enthusiast, subscribing to the plant expeditions of Ludlow and Sherriff, and Kingdon Ward. He planted seedlings from these expeditions which had been propagated in his garden at Bulstrode. Some were tender specimens which thrived in the mild climate of low frost and high rainfall, protected by the shelter of trees. With labour costs increasingly prohibitive, many of the hothouses and Victorian bedding schemes had to go. As the garden sang its swan-song to Lord Muncaster's roses, it became a simpler garden. Having said this, Sir John Ramsden still had at one time thirty-two gardeners to work his seventy-seven acres, whereas now there are only two plus three students.

When 'Patrick of the Hills' and Phyllida were first married he used to spend the afternoons working with her grandfather in the garden. It was from him that he learnt, during the first two years they lived there, about gardening and the garden. 'There are meant to be 643 species of rhododendrons in the world, before you start with the hybrids and although he was quite casual about registering the results, he did produce quite a number which he named after members of his family. The naughtier they were, the further out in the garden they were placed. A great favourite was "Katerina" who

was married to his elder son (later murdered by his cook in Malaya). She was accounted in her youth to be both beautiful and naughty and, like many naughty people, adds greatly to the beauty of life. She was put as far out in the woods as possible with her beautiful great big buff-coloured flowers.'

After Phyllida's grandfather died in 1958 the garden went slightly wild. When I went to interview Patrick, he had just delivered 'Katerina' from the 'bureaucratic authority of the brambles' during his programme of clearance and regeneration. 'We are doing a lot of replanting. We've cut down some of the big, rotten trees and we really ought to cut down an awful lot more. The holes you make need light not wind and working with them you realize what a frail defence there is. We're very lucky because the Gulf Stream hits the coast here. We're sheltered by a big rock of a hill over here from the main west and southwest winds, but the worst wind that we're terrified of is the northeast wind which comes from Birker Moor and is known as the Birker Blow. We're frightened if we pierce anything we'll get into trouble.'

Spending an afternoon with Patrick of the Hills strolling round the garden was, for me, one of the highlights of writing this book. There were plants and places he wanted to show me, so I wired him up to a tape recorder and set off. This is roughly how it went:

How much do you actually do in the garden yourself? 'Very little. I wander around with my secateurs or my loppers. I try quite often to go with the head gardener and decide what we're going to do next. I pick up litter. Actually we're very lucky, we don't get an awful lot.'

He points to the duck pond. 'That's where Joanna the Sarus Crane used to dance. She danced with me on American television. She preferred me to her husband. She was a great catch for the children, eaten by the fox for Christmas a couple of years ago, unfortunately. I've taken the chain-link fence down.'

'And quite a few others, I believe,' I said, having heard he had freed the caged animals previously kept there.

'I don't like to see things in cages. They cost a fortune to keep and the garden was greatly improved by taking the fences down.'

'What about the bears?' I ask.

'Ah, well, that was my mother-in-law's attachment and now I would like to get rid of them, but Phyllida won't hear of it. You know the saying, "If thine enemy offend thee, give him a tame young bear." I met a woman the other day whose son sold bearskins to the army and I got quite excited – no, it's all right. I'm just a great big softie really and anyhow I wouldn't dare.' He took me to a rhododendron with white lily-like trumpets tucked inconscpicuously off the path. 'This is *Rhododendron brachysiphon*. One of my favourite plants in the whole of the garden.'

He pointed to a horse chestnut. 'That's something you mustn't put a rhododendron underneath. The lime in the leaves is much too high, and another piece of useless information, in case you're wanting to get rid of anybody, they're rich in arsenic.'

We came upon a Rousseau-like glade of *Lysichitum*. 'These are

PATRICK IN HIS 'DREAM OF FLOWERS'

....

skunk lilies which absolutely stink but have the most beautiful yellow flowers in spring.' I wanted to photograph him and pointed out the place for him to stand. 'That is the pond, unfortunately,' he said, 'and much as I'd like to oblige you I don't think I'm going to.'

Looking at the photographs later, I reckon he must have got in the swamp after all. But he kept chatting. 'That's a lovely *Eucryphia cordifolia* – once saved my bacon – beautiful plant – flowers at the end of September.

'Oh, we had some senior EEC civil servants here for lunch one day, mostly French, and I greeted them by saying, "We've got a lot of French friends but as a nation you're awful!" They got into a terrible flap until I picked a flower from the *Eucryphia* and put it on all the wives' plates and, after that, they all thought I was marvellous.'

We walked on. 'When I was eight years old my mother brought this ghastly French woman called Mlle Gras with great pebbly spectacles and a large bosom to teach me French. I looked at my sister and my sister looked at me (these royal ferns are rather nice, actually), and we shook our heads and by the following Sunday we had dug a great big pit and we filled it with water and covered it with sticks and leaves. We got her on Sunday and she left on Monday. I'm disgraceful. I don't know what's happened to the *ponticum* this year. We're getting rid of it, and this year it's gone a marvellous dark colour. That *Magnolia delavayii* we picked on 5 December last year. The world has gone very peculiar.'

We reached the Ghyll where the garden opens out on to a well-planted ravine. 'Very nice magnolia, cross-veitchi, when you look at it in the moonlight it's shining white. If you're ever stuck down there, whatever you do, don't grab hold of the *Alaria spinosa*, it's the Devil's Walking Stick – prickly all the way up and down.'

We came out on to the terrace which is a grass walk about half a mile long that follows the contour of the fell and is bordered by a box hedge with yew pillars. The panorama of Eskdale and the Lake District opened out before us. The view had recently

been quite obscured by beech trees but they were cut down in the previous autumn. Still standing is the *Nothofagus obliqua* which was measured as the biggest in Britain.

We veered off the terrace, past Mary Bragg's haunted house, to what he calls 'the dream place', where a large arcade of the rhododendron hybrids is. 'I bring you here because they're just going over. They're the Muncaster hybrids, most of them. Last year there was a small child and her mother walking through here when they were all out – flowers underneath and flowers on the top – and, as they came tripping through, she said "Oh Mummy, isn't it wonderful – it's a dream of flowers!"'

I bade him stand under one of the arching boughs with a hybrid on his head like a Carmen Miranda hat. 'I feel like a proper charlie,' he said. 'I always thought people who took photographs were very difficult. The one who sold Phyllida 120,000 postcards had me standing on top of steps for a whole morning while he waited for the cloud to go over the top. I love this corner really. The camellia behind you is the one we pick on Christmas Day.'

'What do you like best about the garden?' I asked, ignoring his personal remarks. 'Well, it's the feeling really. I suppose it's a feeling of timelessness, life is very short. You come down from the trapstile on a spring evening, you have an awful feeling of time passing you by and yet the garden and the hills are going to be there long after you're gone – some sort of vindication for the human race, I suppose. I'm quite cynical really . . . you probably can't look down just now, but the buttercups at your feet are absolutely wonderful in the sunlight.'

S T A G S H A W

A M B L E S I D E

T his is the last of my gardening tales. I leave you with the wildest, most natural and yet most sophisticated garden in this book, a garden whose creator is no longer alive to tell his story. The gardens of Ruskin, Words- worth, Beatrix Potter were writers' gardens and the owners left us with their thoughts, but here only a few personal recollections of Cubby Acland remain. He had kept a diary called the Stagshaw Diary but it has disappeared. Only the plants speak to us here and tell us of a garden that has been described as one man's obsession.

The garden had its beginnings in Killerton, Devon, the home of the Acland family for generations. Sir Thomas Acland – politician, landowner, philanthropist – began to lay out the garden in the nineteenth century, after the Napoleonic Wars. He was advised by such luminaries as William Robinson, John Coutts and John Veitch who supplemented his expertise with trees and plants from the famous Veitch nurseries nearby, and supplied Killerton with plants grown from seeds and brought back from expeditions to which Sir Thomas subscribed. An arboretum was planted at Killerton on a volcanic hill. It thrived in the rich soil and is one of the best in England today. The success of this garden inspired succeeding generations of the Acland family to add to the collection. It's not difficult to understand how this enthusiasm might after four gen- erations dig itself deep into the Acland psyche. The Aclands, however, didn't collect only for themselves. With their family tradition of liberalism and philanthropy, they became idealistically bound up with the National Trust in its early days and supported its aims to preserve a part of England's heritage through its houses, gardens and countryside. Killerton became one of the first large estates to be handed over to the Trust and it went on to become the Trust's headquarters for that region. Sir Richard's brother, Cubby, went to work for the Trust as a forester and in 1947 his first job was transforming a garden in Godalming. When a job became available in the Lake District he jumped at it. He had had strong links there through his mother's family, the Crop- pers, who own a local paper mill and he had spent many holidays here as a child. The family became more 'spiritually involved with the Lake District,' says Cubby's nephew, Edward, referring to Devon as 'half-way between real country and Hyde Park'.

Ten years after Cubby moved here, Stagshaw became available as a Trust property. He saw the potential to develop the eight acres of woodland behind the house

OVERLOOKING WINDERMERE LAKE

and for the next twenty years until he died this garden was his life. The setting could not have been more perfect for a woodland garden. It rose up steeply, irregularly and dramatically behind the house with various rocky outcroppings and lovely views over Windermere to the Coniston fells. As a spring garden it was unsurpassed. Cubby was a rhododendron fanatic and he envisaged a spring woodland garden of rhododendron, azalea, camellia and magnolia. In this woodland, he had a fifty-year start as the framework of trees was already in place and, with his experience as forester, he knew how to thin the trees and carve out niches and nooks to create glades and vistas. He had his Killerton background and all the expertise of the National Trust available to him, particularly that of Graham Stuart Thomas and Harry Davidian from the Edinburgh Botanical Gardens and greatest living authority on the rhododendron. With this network of contacts, he would have left no rhododendron undiscovered and had no trouble locating a particular specimen.

Cubby Acland had a vision which was not only botanic but artistic. He was interested in the aesthetics of colour. His mother, Eleanor, was a very talented painter and it is likely he would have acquired that particular sensibility from her. He also gained many ideas from Gertrude Jekyll's books. One paints with plants in every garden but he concentrated on individual colour groupings and made it the theme of his garden. These colour groupings were those you might find dabbed on an artist's

TUNNEL OF AZALEAS OVER THE PATH

palette, and he strategically placed them around the garden leading the eye from one to the other, using contrasting foliage in the same way.

The nucleus of Stagshaw, and to my mind its *pièce de résistance*, is the 'painter's palette'. It is set on a plateau and is made of dwarf rhododendrons and Japanese azaleas fused together on a sloping bank, shaped like a painter's palette – including the traditional thumbhole.

Cubby extended the garden gradually, year by year, keeping the trees as a back-drop and striving for a natural look. Into this wilderness went some sophisticated colour schemes in the blending, gradation and groupings of colours. There was the Royal Glade, for instance, where all kinds of purple rhododendrons were planted to-gether according to their particular shades. Up the long path are the *Griersonianum* hybrids associated by parentage in red and orange colours. In other parts of the garden pinks and reds appear together, or groupings of white, yellow and cream. The azaleas start at the bottom of the hill with pastel shades and finish at the top with fiery reds.

In and amongst these little pockets of colour schemes are the beautiful strong trees of the woodland, but also the specimen trees such as the snowdrop tree, the tulip tree, the pocket handkerchief tree, and eucryphias, eucalyptus, magnolias and the Chilean fire bush. Interesting foliage contrasts, counterpoints or blends with the acers, *Corylus maxima* 'Purpurea' and pieris.

The fifth dimension in this garden is its depth – you look over, under, across, up, down, into and out of so many standpoints in the garden that it becomes a garden of perspective. This was achieved by a clever manipulation of trees and the genius of a geometrist. It is particularly effective as not only did the points of view have to work compositionally, but colourwise as well.

By the time Cubby died, he had painted his five-dimensional canvas with 300 species and hybrids of rhododendron as well as fifty to sixty azaleas. 'He understood what plants needed and how to manipulate them,' says Edward Acland. Edward often visited his uncle for tea when Cubby would take him around the garden to show him the colour schemes. 'See how carefully I've chosen them,' Cubby would say.

Keith Thompkinson came in 1977 to help with the garden and stayed on for a few years after Cubby died. He described the creation of the moss garden on a high rocky outcropping at the top of the garden. Mosses had grown there naturally and Cubby and Keith tried everything to get rid of them but the mosses kept coming back. Finally they gave up and encouraged them. Cubby had seen moss gardens in Japan and wrote to them asking how to go about starting one. The Japanese sent plans using beds of gravel, a plastic sheet and peat sand. The moss garden was a great success with all the mosses meeting together. The Wordsworths would have been delighted.

Keith describes Cubby as a grand old character, an old-fashioned country squire, a great British eccentric. In the summer he would stand in his shorts swinging away with an old scythe singing 'All Things Bright and Beautiful'. A favourite anecdote is recounted when some friends arrived at his house for a meeting to find him standing with his gardening apron on top of a stepladder with a long-handled fungicide brush vigorously scrubbing the bark of a four-stemmed birch tree known as 'White Ladies' to get the algae off and make her shiny. He turned round to his assembled guests saying, 'This is the only time you'll ever catch me scrubbing a lady's back with a bath brush'. His garden was like an exotic mistress. He dressed her in sublimely coloured frocks of rhododendron, embothriums, camellias, eucryphias and magnolias, cloaked her in foliage and adorned her with the delicate baubles of snowdrops, primroses, bluebells and carpets of *Cornus canadensis*.

Continuity of the family gardening tradition was very important to him and he achieved this in creating what has been called a 'mini Killerton' at Stagshaw. He often spoke of the old head gardener there who had taught him so much. In his garden as in his life, Cubby was known for taking a view and sticking to it – outspoken, forthright but gentle. Passionate about trees, in his twenty-two years as Regional Agent for the National Trust he planted much of the Windermere shoreline owned by the Trust.

Unfortunately, he didn't grow deaf with age. He was a great sailor, Commodore of

the Yacht Club, and introduced dinghy sailing to Windermere. Edward says that the noise of the speedboats on his lake became louder every year and spoilt the garden for him. He had devoted his whole life to creating an aesthetic paradise and was defeated by the invisible.

The garden was open to the public when Cubby was alive and happily for us will remain so. As with all gardens, for the garden to continue exactly as Cubby left it, a clone would have to be found, and time stand still. Everything grows at such an alarming rate here that garden visions soon lose their focus. The view of the lake is rather obscured now by the growth of trees. But plans are afoot to restore the garden, Cubby's garden. To me he represents the most imaginative gardener – the kind that dreams as artists dream.

THE PAINTER'S PALETTE OF JAPANESE AZALEAS

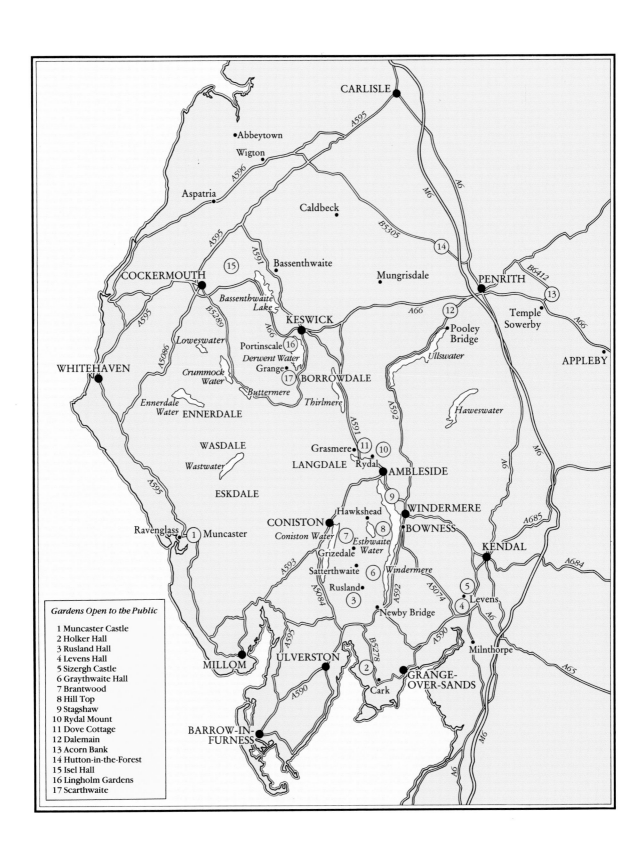

Gardens Open to the Public

1 Muncaster Castle
2 Holker Hall
3 Rusland Hall
4 Levens Hall
5 Sizergh Castle
6 Graythwaite Hall
7 Brantwood
8 Hill Top
9 Stagshaw
10 Rydal Mount
11 Dove Cottage
12 Dalemain
13 Acorn Bank
14 Hutton-in-the-Forest
15 Isel Hall
16 Lingholm Gardens
17 Scarthwaite

A Guide to the Gardens Open to the Public

In order to keep the essays on each garden as atmospheric as possible – and primarily in English – I have asked each head gardener or owner to list separately here a few plants they feel have a special botanical or historical interest or which are personal favourites. This list is by no means a comprehensive list of all the plants in each garden. Details of visiting times and other useful information are also listed.

The gardens are grouped by area and, although most of them serve teas, cakes and sandwiches, three are worth visiting at lunchtime for their excellent food. They are: Dalemain near Penrith; Levens near Kendal and Brantwood in Coniston. Holker, Dalemain, Levens and Muncaster Castle are especially good for a day out with children.

Don't attempt any of these gardens in stiletto heels and take a tip from my husband, who never leaves home without an umbrella.

Gardens In The North

Acorn Bank,
Temple Sowerby, Penrith
The National Trust
(05394) 33883

Garden open Easter to the end of October, 10 to 6 every day. 'Meet the Gardener' days approximately once a month during the season. Shop. Plants for sale. Paths and lavatories suitable for disabled. Special access to greenhouse. Free parking for cars and coaches. Comprehensive collection of over 200 herbs.

SELECTED PLANTS:

Aesculus×mutablis 'Induta'	*Hydrangea arborescens*
Anemone nemorosa 'Vestal'	'Grandiflora'
Baptisia australis	*Indigofera gerardiana*
Chaenomeles speciosa	*Kirengeshoma palmata*
'Moerloosei'	*Lysimachia ephemerum*
Clematis×jouiniana	*Mahonia lomariifolia* (if it
Clematis rehderana	survives the cold)
Clematis viticella (in	*Ranunculus bulbosus*
variety)	'Pleniflorus'
Dictamnus albus	*Rosa bracteata* (the best)
Dill (a most beautiful	*Rosa webbiana*
cure for flatulence)	*Tulipa sylvestris* (Britain's
Erythronium americanum	native tulip)
Euphorbia polychroma	*Veratrum album*
Gillenia trifoliata	*Veratrum viride*

Dalemain, Dacre,
Penrith
(08536) 450

House and garden open Easter Sunday to mid-October, 11.15 to 5. Closed Fridays and Saturdays. Guided tours around garden with specialist available by arrangement. Licensed restaurant serves lunches and afternoon teas (recommended). Shop, adventure playground, Craft Fair in July. Coach and car parking. Suitable for disabled who are admitted free. Collection of daffodils and narcissus 'Old' and shrub roses of many kinds especially 'Céleste/'Celestial', old China, *R. hugonis*, and undiscovered ones as well.

SELECTED PLANTS:

Agapanthus	(George Sherriff's)
Brunnera macrophylla	Mints of various species
'Variegata'	Tree peonies
Fagus silvatica 'Fastigiata'	*Primula alpicola violacea*
(Dawyck beech) and fern-	Revd. Robert's gold-
leaved beeches	edged white 'rock'
Geraniums esp. *G.*	from Martindale
macrorrhizum 'Walter	*Phygelius capensis* (Cape
Ingwerson'	figwort)
Iris chrysographes	*Silene barbata*
Iris chrysographes rubella	*Smilacinea racemosa*
Ligularia przewalskii	*Tropaeolum speciosum*
Ligularia tangutica	*Veratrum album*
Meconopsis grandis G.S. 600	

Hutton-in-the-Forest,
Penrith
(08534) 449

Garden open all year, 11 to 5. House and tea room open 1 – 4 on Bank Holiday Mondays and Thursdays, Fridays and Sundays during summer. Check for details. Woodland walk. Partly suitable for wheelchairs. Coach parties welcome. Ample parking. Old espalier fruit trees in the walled garden.

SELECTED PLANTS:

Abies concolor lowiana	*Picea sitchensis*
Abies grandis	*Populus* (several varieties)
Cercidiphyllum japonicum	*Quercus robur*
Fagus sylvatica	*Sequoiadendron giganteum*
Galanthus	*Tilia platyphyllos*
Nothofagus obliqua	*Tsuga heterophylla*
Nothofagus procera	*Veratrum nigrum*
Papaver	

Isel Hall,
near Cockermouth

Open by written appointment. Fairly suitable for wheelchairs. Parking. Ten beds of herbaceous plants.

SELECTED PLANTS:

Clematis
Cranesbills
Lambs' ears
Lavender
Lilies
Peonies
Quinces
Rock roses

Rosa 'Maigold'
Siberian crab apples
Wild cherries
Wild poppies and
marguerites
Wisteria from Persia
Yew

Lingholm Gardens, Keswick (07687) 72003

Garden open 1 April to 31 October 10 to 5. Special parties can have guided tours by arrangement. Coach parties by arrangement only. Tea room for light lunchtime snacks and afternoon teas. Plant centre for hardy and greenhouse plants. Car park. Suitable for disabled. 'Wheelchair' walk, toilets, ramps. Spring daffodils, **large species rhododendron collection**.

SELECTED PLANTS AND TREES:

Abies nordmanniana
Cedrus atlantica 'Glauca'
Cercidiphyllum japonicum
Embothrium coccineum
Eucryphia glutinosa
Fagus sylvatica 'Laciniata'
Gentiana sini ornata
Magnolia acuminata

Meconopsis grandis
Parrotia persica
Picea abies (tallest)
Primulas (candelabra
type)
Sequoiadendron giganteum
Tropaeolum speciosum

Scarthwaite, Grange-in-Borrowdale Mrs Nan Hicks

Open throughout season for National Gardens Scheme, see their Yellow Book for details. Teas in village nearby. Not suitable for wheelchairs. No parking.

SELECTED PLANTS:

Arum italicum 'Pictum'
Clematis alpina
Clematis macropetala
Clematis macropetala
'Markham's Pink'
Eryngium alpinum
Euphorbia wallichii
Ferns – *Adiantum pedatum*
Asplenium scolopendrium
'Crispum'
Athyrium nipponicum
'Pictum'
Dryopteris affinis dilitata
crispa 'Whiteside'

Osmunda regalis
Galanthus nivalis 'Sam
Arnott'
Hosta fortunei 'Albopicta'
Hosta sieboldiana 'Frances
Williams'
Iris innominata
Orcis (Dactylorrhiza) foliosa
Smilacina racemosa
Stipa gigantea
Tricyrtis formosana
stolonifera
Viola cornuta

GARDENS IN THE SOUTH

Sizergh Castle, Kendal The National Trust (05395) 60070

Garden open Easter to end October on Sunday, Monday, Wednesday, and Thursday afternoons from 2

to 6 but check before visiting. 'Meet the Gardener' days approximately once a month throughout season. Great Sizergh Plant Sale held in May. Teas, shop. Wheelchairs can get around garden but there are no other special facilities for disabled people. Car and coach park. Reduced fees for parties of 15 or more by arrangement with administrator.

SELECTED PLANTS:

Asplenium scolopendrium
'Crispum'
Aster frikartii 'Mönch'
Athyrium filix femina
'Victoriae'
Athyrium nipponicum
'Pictum'
Buddleia lindleyana
Buddleia weyerana
'Moonlight'
Cercidiphyllum japonicum
Clematis rehderana
Cupressus lawsoniana
'Wisselii'
Cyclamen coum
Davidia involucrata
Dryopteris erythrosora
Dryopteris wallichiana
Echinacea angustifolia
Epilobium glabellum
Epimedium×rubrum
Eucryphia×nymansensis
'Nymansay'

Gentiana asclepiadea
Helleborus viridis
Hydrangea sargentiana
Lilium 'Bellingham
hybrids'
Pulmonaria angustifolia
'Azurea'
Phyteuma nigra
Primula capitata
'Mooreana'
Primula elatior
Primula viallii
Ramonda myconi
Ribes speciosum
Rosa alba 'Céleste'/
'Celestial'
Rosa omeiensis
Roscoea cautleoides
Rudbeckia deamii
Sciadopitys verticillata
Syringa×josiflexa 'Bellicent'
Tsuga canadensis 'Pendula'

Levens Hall, Kendal (05395) 60321

House and garden open Easter Sunday to 30 September on Sundays to Thursdays 11 to 5 (last entry to house at 4.30). Closed Fridays and Saturdays. Guided tours with head gardener once a month throughout the season. Steam collection 2 to 5 Sunday to Thursday. Licensed cafeteria serving light lunches and homemade teas. Gift shop, children's play area. Garden suitable for wheelchairs. Coach parties by arrangement. Ample parking. Ring for further details. Topiary of box and yew. Beech hedge.

SELECTED PLANTS:

Actinidia chinensis
Actinidia kolomikta
Anchusa 'Blue Bird'
Anemone japonicum
Cerciphyllum japonicum
Cheiranthus 'Bowles
Mauve'
Chrysanthemum foeniculare
Chrysanthemum fruticosum
'Jamaica Primrose'
Cosmos
Diascia rigescens
Eryngium 'Miss Willmott's

Ghost'
Ginkgo biloba
Heliotrope
Hydrangea sargentiana
Hydrangea villosa
Metasequoia glyptostroboides
Nicotiana langsdorfii
Roses
Sidalcea
Tropaeolum speciosum
Verbena venosa
Wisteria chinensis

Holker Hall,
Cark-in-Cartmel,
Grange-over-Sands
(044853) 328

Open Easter Sunday to the last Sunday in October daily except Saturday, 10.30 to 6. Last admission to grounds and hall 4.30. Park open until 6. Facilities for the disabled. Lakeland Motor Museum, Craft and Countryside Museum, Discovery Walks, Baby Animal House, Historic Kitchen Exhibition, cafeteria and gift shop. Ample parking.

SELECTED PLANTS:

Abutilon vitifolium 'Album'	*Osmanthus yunnanensis*
Amelanchier asiatica	*Oxydendrum arboreum*
Buddleia alternifolia	*Prunus* 'Shimidsu Sakura'
'Argentea'	*Rhododendron concinnum*
Cercidiphyllum japonicum	*pseudoyanthinum*
Cornus controversa	*Rhododendron hodgsonii*
Cornus nuttallii 'Monarch'	*Schisandra grandiflora*
Emmenopterys henryi	*rubriflora*
Eucryphia glutinosa	*Stewartia koreana*
Lindera obtusiloba	*Stewartia malacodendron*
Magnolia denudata	*Stewartia pseudocamellia*
Magnolia hypoleuca	

GARDENS IN THE WEST

Muncaster Castle,
Ravenglass
(06577) 203/614

Garden open 12 to 5, House open 1.30 to 4.30 Good Friday to 30 September but not on Mondays, except Bank Holidays. Tea room, shop. Suitable for wheelchairs. Coaches by appointment. Ample parking. Numerous camellias, acers, hydrangeas and azaleas.

SELECTED PLANTS:

Aralia spinosa	*Rhododendron hookeri*
Castanea sativa (sweet chestnut at front door reputed to be 600 years old)	*Rhododendron johnstoneanum*
	Rhododendron macabeanum
	Rhododendron mallotum
	Rhododendron megacalyx
Eucryphia cordifolia	*Rhododendron moupinense*
Magnolia wilsonii	*Rhododendron protistum*
Nothofagus betuloides	*Rhododendron tephropeplum*
Nothofagus obliqua	*Rhododendron tsariense*
Populus wilsonii (given to Sir John by Emperor of Japan from his own garden)	*Rhododendron williamsianum*
	Rhododendron×'Aladdin'
	Rhododendron×'Hawk Crest'
Pseudotsuga taxifolia (Douglas fir planted from seed from Murthly in Perthshire in 1871)	*Rhododendron×*'Joan Ramsden'
	Rhododendron×'Margaret Findlay'
Rhododendron beantanum	*Rhododendron×*'Muncaster Mist'
Rhododendron brachysiphon	*Rhododendron×*'Sunrise'
Rhododendron callimorphum	*Sciadopitys verticiellata* (Japanese umbrella tree)
Rhododendron falconeri	
Rhododendron griersonianum	

CENTRAL GARDENS

Brantwood,
Coniston
(05394) 41396

Open daily mid-March to mid-November 11 – 5.30. Winter season Wednesday to Sunday 11 – 4. Light lunches (recommended) and teas available at licensed restaurant. Lakeland Craft Guild shop, Wainwright exhibition, nature trail, book shop. Steam yacht 'Gondola' stops at the pier. Ample parking.

SELECTED PLANTS:

Acer griseum	*Meconopsis betonicifolia*
Acer palmatum var.	*Meconopsis cambrica*
Acer pectinatum	*Meconopsis nepaulensis*
Amelanchier canadensis	*Meconopsis regia*
Arisarum proboscideum	*Metasequoia glyptostroboides*
Artemesia stellerana	*Microbiota decussata*
Azalea (various old hybrids)	*Narcissus species* (planted by Ruskin)
Azalea luteum (glorious)	*Nothofagus antarctica*
Azalea schlippenbachii	*Paulownia tomentosa*
Camellia 'Elegans'	*Picea breweriana*
Camellia×williamsii hybrids	*Rhododendron arboreum*
	Rhododendron dichroanthum
Cornus kousa chinensis	*Rhododendron fulvum*
Desfontainea spinosa	*Rhododendron litiense*
Eucryphia×nymansensis 'Nymansay'	*Rhododendron montroseanum*
	Rhododendron thomsonii
Garrya elliptica	*Rhododendron* 'Loderi' group
Gentiana (various)	
Hamamelis mollis	*Rhododendron* 'Luscombei'
Hydrangea aspera	*Rhododendron* "Faggetter's Favourite'
Hydrangea macrophylla	
Hydrangea paniculata	*Rhododendron* 'Fastuosum Flore Pleno'
Hydrangea villosa	
Lilium candidum	Old roses (Musks, Gallicas, Moss, Damasks, etc.)
Lilium regale	
Magnolia sieboldii	
Magnolia grandiflora 'Exmouth'	*Schizostylis coccinea* 'Major'

Dove Cottage,
Grasmere
(09665) 544/547

Open 9.30 to 5.30 in summer, 9.30 to dusk in winter. Museum, gift shop. Teas nearby. Small car park.

SELECTED PLANTS:

Berberis	Perennial sweet pea
Bog primula	Portugal laurel
Cowslips	Primroses
Daffodils (small, 'lent lilies' is local name)	Ragged robin
	Rugosa rose with honeysuckle
Dog's tooth violets	
Ferns (various)	Violets
Foxgloves	Westmorland damson
Fritillaria	Wild pansies
Lenten rose	Wood anemone
Melancholy thistle	Wood sorrel
Mosses	Yews (planted by Wordsworth)
Mullein	

Graythwaite Hall,
Hawkshead
(05395) 31333

Garden open 10 to 6, daily 1 April to 30 June. Fairly
suitable for wheelchairs.

SELECTED PLANTS:

Acer griseum	*Euonymous alatus*
Acer japonicum 'Aureum'	*Hydrangea sargentiana*
Acer senkaki	*Liquidambar styraciflua*
Acer vitifolium	*Malus hupehensis*
Acer tschonskii	*Malus tschonoskii*
Aesculus×carnea 'Briottii'	*Populus candicans* 'Aurora'
Azalea 'Christina'	*Prunus serrula*
Azalea 'Jean Weeks'	*Rhododendron keysii*
Azalea komiamae	*Rhododendron fancium*
Azalea mucronatum	*Rhododendron* 'Bali'
Azalea tschonskii	*Rhododendron* 'Ben
Camellia 'Brigadoon'	Moseley'
Camellia williamsii	*Rhododendron* 'Daphnoides'
Desfontainia spinosa	

Hill Top,
Sawrey
The National Trust
(09666) 269

Open Monday to Wednesday, Saturday and Sunday
10–5. Very crowded at peak holiday times. Best visited
in May, June, September or October. Shop. Parking 100
yards, unsuitable for coaches. Unsuitable for disabled
visitors but visually handicapped with guide dogs
welcome. The vegetable garden will be opened to
visitors by the beginning of 1990.

SELECTED PLANTS:

Plants thought to	*Chrysanthemum*
originate from Beatrix	*leucanthemum*
Potter's time:	*Enkianthus campanulatus*
Chaenomeles japonica	*Rosa* 'Albéric Barbier'
Eucryphia glutinosa	*Rosa* 'American Pillar'
Pinus sylvestris	*Rosa* 'Leverkusen'
Wisteria sinensis 'Alba'	*Verbascum thapsus*
	Vitis vinifera 'Brandt'
Other interesting plants:	
Angelica archangelica	

Rusland Hall,
Rusland,
near Newby Bridge
(022984) 276

Open by telephone appointment. Parking.

SELECTED PLANTS:

Cedar of Lebanon	200-year-old magnolia
2 ginkgo trees (one being	Rare yellow
the largest specimen in	rhododendron
Cumbria)	Ancient yew
Lilac	

Rydal Mount,
Rydal
(05394) 33002

House and garden open 1 March to 31 October 9.30
to 5. 1 November to end February 10 to 4. Closed
Tuesdays in winter. Shop, car park. Naturalized
bluebells and daffodils and many herbaceous plants.

SELECTED PLANTS:

Acer palmatum	*Fraxinus*
Betula	*Halesia*
Ceanothus	*Hydrangea*
Clematis montana	*Jasminum nudiflorum*
Cryptomeria japonica	*Laburnum*
Deutzia	*Magnolia*
Enkianthus	*Philadelphus*
Eucryphia	*Pinus sylvestris*
Exochorda racemosa	*Symphoricarpos*
Fagus sylvatica	*Taxus baccata* 'Aurea'
'Heterophylla'	*Thuya plicata*
Fuchsia magellanica	*Weigela*
'Riccartonii'	*Wisteria*

Stagshaw,
Ambleside
The National Trust
(05394) 32109

Garden open from April to end June, every day from 10
to 6. July to end October by appointment. Parking
not suitable for coaches, no lavatories. Garden not suitable
for wheelchairs. Wear sensible shoes and stay on paths.
Japanese and *occidentale* azaleas, dwarf rhododendrons,
species and hybrid rhododendrons including *triflorums*
and *griersonianum* hybrids.

SELECTED PLANTS:

Acer palmatum 'Senkaki'	*Liriodendron*
Acer pensylvanicum	*Magnolia cylindrica*
'Erythrocladum'	*Magnolia kobus stellata*
Cornus canadensis	*Magnolia salicifolia*
Corylus maxima 'Purpurea'	*Magnolia sieboldii*
Davidia	*Magnolia sinensis*
Embothrium	*Magnolia wilsonii*
Erythronium	*Metasequoia glyptostroboides*
Eucalyptus	*Pieris forrestii*
Eucryphia	*Rhus typhina*
Griselinia littoralis	*Rosa longicuspis*
Halesia	*Rosa synstyae*